BE

ALIVE

BE

ALIVE

GET TO KNOW THE LIVING SAVIOR

NT COMMENTARY

JOHN 1—12

Warren W. Wiersbe

David C Cook®

transforming lives together

BE ALIVE
Published by David C Cook
4050 Lee Vance View
Colorado Springs, CO 80918 U.S.A.

David C Cook Distribution Canada
55 Woodslee Avenue, Paris, Ontario, Canada N3L 3E5

David C Cook U.K., Kingsway Communications
Eastbourne, East Sussex BN23 6NT, England

The graphic circle C logo is a registered trademark of David C Cook.

Unless otherwise noted, all Scripture quotations are taken from the King James Version of the Bible.
(Public Domain.) Scripture quotations marked NASB are taken from the New American Standard
Bible, © Copyright 1960, 1995 by The Lockman Foundation. Used by permission; PH are taken
from J. B. Phillips: *The New Testament in Modern English*, revised editions © J. B. Phillips, 1958,
1960, 1972, permission of Macmillan Publishing Co. and Collins Publishers; NKJV are taken from
the New King James Version. Copyright © 1982 by Thomas Nelson, Inc. Used by permission. All
rights reserved. Italics in Scripture have been added by the author for emphasis; and NIV are taken
from the *Holy Bible, New International Version®. NIV®*. Copyright © 1973, 1978, 1984
International Bible Society. Used by permission of Zondervan. All rights reserved.

LCCN 2008937090
ISBN 978-1-4347-6736-3
eISBN 978-1-4347-0299-9

© 1986 Warren W. Wiersbe

First edition of *Be Alive* by Warren W. Wiersbe published by Victor Books®
in 1986 © Warren W. Wiersbe, ISBN 978-0-89693-359-0

The Team: Karen Lee-Thorp, Amy Kiechlin, Jack Campbell, and Susan Vannaman
Series Cover Design: John Hamilton Design
Cover Photo: Corbis Corporation

Printed in the United States of America
Second Edition 2009

7 8 9 10 11 12

083112

To some younger friends in the ministry who have been a joy and an encouragement to my wife, Betty, and me:

Mark and Cindy Brunott
Dana and Christa Olson
Mike and Anne Wagner

CONTENTS

THE BIG IDEA

An Introduction to *Be Alive*
by Ken Baugh

Here's a question for you to ponder: *"What is the most important thing you will not be able to do in heaven?"* C'mon, think about it—don't just skip ahead to find the answer, really think about it for a minute. *"What is the most important thing you cannot do in heaven?"*

Give up? I think the answer is simply this: "I will not be able to be an evangelist in heaven." You may not have ever thought about this before, but sharing the faith with unbelievers is the number one thing we can do here on earth that we will not be able to do in heaven.

So how are you doing in your evangelistic efforts? When was the last time you told someone about Jesus? When was the last time you opened your door to a Jehovah's Witness or Mormon to share with them the real Jesus of the Bible? When was the last time you pulled out your Bible on an airplane hoping that the person next to you would become curious enough to ask you a question about it? Feeling guilty yet? Yeah, me too—and I'm a pastor. I don't know about you, but when I get on an airplane I often hide behind my iPod and put a disinterested look on my face.

In 2004, The Barna Group asked a number of Christians how many times they had shared their faith in the past year, and they discovered that of those surveyed, only 49 percent said that they had done so. Wow, less than half! Is it any wonder why more people are not becoming Christians? The truth is that God has chosen you and me to share the gospel with others, and if we neglect to make the most of every opportunity to share our faith, people won't hear the gospel. And if they don't hear the gospel, they can't make a decision for Christ, and if they never make a decision for Christ, they will die in their sins, and if they die in their sins, they will be separated from God for eternity in a very real place of torment called hell.

I know I'm laying it on kind of thick right now, but don't you think this is important? John definitely thought so, so much so that the Big Idea that runs through the first twelve chapters of his gospel is dedicated to presenting Jesus as the divine Son of God. John's gospel is different from the Synoptics in that there is no genealogy, no account of Christ's birth, nothing about His temptation in the wilderness, no mention of the transfiguration, no mention of how Jesus went about appointing His disciples, no parables, no account of His ascension, and no reference to the Great Commission. Instead, John emphasizes that Jesus is the Creator, the only begotten of the Father, the Lamb of God who takes away the sins of the world, and even the "I AM" of Exodus 3:14. But, John emphasizes more than any of the other gospel writers that Jesus is the divine Son of God. And John makes it very clear that any person who does not believe in Jesus as the divine Son of God is condemned: "Whoever does not believe stands condemned already because he has not believed in the name of God's one and only Son" (John 3:18 NIV).

Now, you may be thinking to yourself right now: *Ken, I don't have the gift of evangelism. Isn't it okay for me to just defer this whole evangelism task to others who do?* Well, the short answer to that question is NO. It's true that some Christians do have the gift of evangelism, but that doesn't let the rest of us who don't off the hook. (Yeah, I'm a pastor who doesn't have the gift of evangelism. Go figure.) The fact is, whether we're comfortable with it or not, the mandate of the Great Commission is for every believer to go and "make disciples," and of course the very first step to a person becoming a disciple is that they make a decision to believe that Jesus is the divine Son of God.

So why is it so difficult to be an evangelist? What are the obstacles that get in the way? I think there are two.

The first obstacle is what I call the lack-of-knowledge barrier. This is when the person (maybe you) doesn't think they know enough about the Bible or theology to effectively answer people's questions. The second obstacle is the fear barrier (I thought that one might ring a bell). Many of us are terrified of the opposition that often ensues with evangelistic efforts. But I'm convinced that every believer can overcome these two barriers and effectively share their faith. Let me show you how.

I believe the most effective way to overcome the lack-of-knowledge barrier is to focus your witnessing opportunity on Jesus' personal testimony of His divine nature. This is the Big Idea of John 1—12. How many times have you heard someone say "Oh, I believe Jesus lived, and I believe He was a good moral teacher, but I certainly do not believe He *was* God, and I don't believe He ever said He was"? Well, the truth is, Jesus did claim to be God, and there are many examples recorded in John's gospel. Let me show you one in chapter 10.

Jesus asked the Jews why they were about to stone Him. He said, "'I have shown you many great miracles from the Father. For which of these do you stone me?' 'We are not stoning you for any of these,' replied the Jews, 'but for blasphemy, because you, a mere man, claim to be God'" (John 10:31–33 niv). Here we see how John used Jesus' personal testimony of His divine nature as a tool for evangelism. Why? Because, when a person is faced with the evidence of Jesus' divine status and hears it from His own lips, they have to make a decision: Is Jesus divine or not? I think C. S. Lewis captures the essence of this issue succinctly when he says,

> A man who was merely a man and said the sort of things Jesus said would not be a great moral teacher. He would either be a lunatic—on a level with the man who says he is a poached egg—or else he would be the Devil of Hell. You must make your choice. Either this man was, and is, the Son of God: or else a madman or something worse. You can shut Him up for a fool, you can spit at Him and kill Him as a demon; or you can fall at His feet and call Him Lord and God. But let us not come with any patronizing nonsense about His being a great human teacher. He has not left that open to us. He did not intend to.
>
> —C. S. Lewis, *Mere Christianity*

Therefore, one of the most effective ways to overcome the lack-of-knowledge barrier is to do what John did: Focus your conversation on Jesus' testimony of Himself as God in human flesh. This is the quickest means of getting to the heart of the gospel message.

Second, I believe that the most effective way to overcome the fear barrier is to remember that *your job is not to convert anyone.* That's God's job. Your responsibility as an evangelist is simply to scatter seeds of truth that reveal the person and work of Christ. Scatter the various seeds of truth in regard to Jesus' deity (see John 1:1–3; Col. 1:15–17; 2:9; and Heb. 1:3), and scatter the various seeds of truth that reveal what Jesus came to do (see John 3:16–18).

The Big Idea in chapters 1—12 of John's gospel is that Jesus is the divine Son of God, and the most effective way to share this truth is to share Jesus' testimony about Himself. Do it boldly as you recognize that your job is simply to scatter the seeds of truth about Christ's person and work and nothing else. God's Word does not return void:

> As the rain and the snow come down from heaven, and do not return to it without watering the earth and making it bud and flourish, so that it yields seed for the sower and bread for the eater, so is my word that goes out from my mouth: It will not return to me empty, but will accomplish what I desire and achieve the purpose for which I sent it. (Isa. 55:10–11 NIV)

***

Dr. Wiersbe's commentaries have been a source of guidance and strength to me over the many years that I have been a pastor. His unique style is not overly academic, but theologically sound. He explains the deep truths of Scripture in a way that everyone can understand and apply. Whether you're a Bible scholar or a brand-new believer in Christ, you will benefit, as I have, from Warren's insights. With your Bible in one hand and Dr. Wiersbe's commentary in the other, you will be able to accurately unpack the deep truths of God's Word and learn how to apply them to your life.

Drink deeply, my friend, of the truths of God's Word, for in them you will find Jesus Christ, and there is freedom, peace, assurance, and joy.

—Ken Baugh
Pastor of Coast Hills Community Church
Aliso Viejo, California

A Word from the Author

During the months that I have been studying the gospel of John and writing this book, I have felt like a man standing on holy ground. The more I studied and wrote, the more inadequate I felt. No wonder the great Greek scholar Dr. A. T. Robertson called the gospel of John "the profoundest book in the world."

There is not space in these studies to plumb the depths, but I have tried to present the basic teachings of this marvelous book. The gospel of John is simple enough for a child to wade in, but deep enough for the scholar and the most seasoned saint to swim in.

This book is the first of two volumes devoted to the gospel of John. The second one, *Be Transformed*, focuses on chapters 13—21.

Please come to this book with the heart and mind of a worshipper. John did not simply write a book; he painted exciting pictures. These pages are filled with images such as the Lamb, the Door, the Shepherd, the new birth, the light and darkness, the Water of Life, bread, blindness, seeds, and dozens more. Use your "sanctified imagination" as you study, and the gospel of John will become a new book to you.

And, remember, you are not studying a book—you are seeing a person. "And we beheld his glory … full of grace and truth" (John 1:14).

—Warren W. Wiersbe

A SUGGESTED OUTLINE OF THE BOOK OF JOHN

Theme: Jesus is the Christ; believe and live!

Key verse: John 20:31

I. Opportunity (John 1:15—6:71)

    He presents Himself to …

    A. His disciples (John 1:19—2:12)

    B. The Jews (John 2:13—3:36)

    C. The Samaritans (John 4:1–54)

    D. The Jewish leaders (John 5:1–47)

    E. The multitudes (John 6:1–71)

II. Opposition (John 7—12)

    There is conflict with the Jewish leaders over …

    A. Moses (John 7:1—8:11)

    B. Abraham (John 8:12–59)

    C. Who Messiah is (John 9:1—10:42)

    D. His miraculous power (John 11:1—12:36)

    E. They would not believe in Him (John 12:37–50)

III. Outcome (John 13—21)

    A. The faith of the disciples (John 13—17)

    B. The unbelief of the Jews (John 18—19)

    C. The victory of Christ (John 20—21)

Chapter One

GOD IS HERE!

(John 1)

B ut will God indeed dwell on the earth?" asked Solomon as he dedicated the temple (1 Kings 8:27). A good question, indeed! God's glory had dwelled in the tabernacle (Ex. 40:34) and in the temple (1 Kings 8:10–11), but that glory had departed from disobedient Israel (Ezek. 9:3; 10:4, 18; 11:22–23).

Then a marvelous thing happened: The glory of God came to His people again, in the person of His Son, Jesus Christ. The writers of the four gospels have given us "snapshots" of our Lord's life on earth, for no complete biography could ever be written (John 21:25). Matthew wrote with his fellow Jews in mind and emphasized that Jesus of Nazareth had fulfilled the Old Testament prophecies. Mark wrote for the busy Romans. Whereas Matthew emphasized the King, Mark presented the Servant, ministering to needy people. Luke wrote his gospel for the Greeks and introduced them to the sympathetic Son of Man.

But it was given to John, the beloved disciple, to write a book for both Jews and Gentiles, presenting Jesus as the Son of God. We know that John had Gentiles in mind as well as Jews, because he often "interpreted" Jewish words or customs for his readers (John 1:38, 41–42; 5:2; 9:7; 19:13, 17;

20:16). His emphasis to the Jews was that Jesus not only fulfilled the Old Testament prophecies but also fulfilled the *types*. Jesus is the Lamb of God (John 1:29) and the Ladder from heaven to earth (John 1:51; and see Gen. 28). He is the New Temple (John 2:19–21), and He gives a new birth (John 3:4ff.). He is the serpent lifted up (John 3:14) and the Bread of God that came down from heaven (John 6:35ff.).

Whereas the first three gospels major on describing *events* in the life of Christ, John emphasized the *meaning* of these events. For example, all four gospels record the feeding of the five thousand, but only John records Jesus' sermon on "The Bread of Life," which followed that miracle when He interpreted it for the people.

But there is one major theme that runs throughout John's gospel: Jesus Christ is the Son of God, and if you commit yourself to Him, He will give you eternal life (John 20:31). In this first chapter, John recorded seven names and titles of Jesus that identify Him as eternal God.

1. THE WORD (1:1–3, 14)

Much as our words reveal to others our hearts and minds, so Jesus Christ is God's "Word" to reveal His heart and mind to us. "He that hath seen me hath seen the Father" (John 14:9). A word is composed of letters, and Jesus Christ is "Alpha and Omega" (Rev. 1:11), the first and last letters of the Greek alphabet. According to Hebrews 1:1–3, Jesus Christ is God's *last* Word to mankind, for He is the climax of divine revelation.

Jesus Christ is the eternal Word (vv. 1–2). He existed in the beginning, not because He had a beginning as a creature, but because He is eternal. He *is* God and He was *with* God. "Before Abraham was, I am" (John 8:58).

Jesus Christ is the creative Word (v. 3). There is certainly a parallel between John 1:1 and Genesis 1:1, the "new creation" and the "old creation." God created the worlds through His word: "And God said, 'Let there be …'"/ "For he spake, and it was done; he commanded, and it stood fast" (Ps. 33:9). God created all things through Jesus Christ (Col. 1:16), which means that Jesus is not a created being. He is eternal God.

The verb *was made* is perfect tense in the Greek, which means a "completed act." Creation is finished. It is not a process still going on, even though God is certainly at work in His creation (John 5:17). Creation is not a process; it is a finished product.

Jesus Christ is the incarnate Word (v. 14). He was not a phantom or a spirit when He ministered on earth, nor was His body a mere illusion. John and the other disciples each had a personal experience that convinced them of the reality of the body of Jesus (1 John 1:1–2). Even though John's emphasis is the deity of Christ, he makes it clear that the Son of God came *in the flesh* and was subject to the sinless infirmities of human nature.

In his gospel, John points out that Jesus was weary (John 4:6) and thirsty (John 4:7), that He groaned within (John 11:33) and openly wept (John 11:35). On the cross, He thirsted (John 19:28), died (John 19:30), and bled (John 19:34). After His resurrection, He proved to Thomas and the other disciples that He still had a real body (John 20:24–29), howbeit, a glorified body.

How was the "Word made flesh"? By the miracle of the virgin birth (Isa. 7:14; Matt. 1:18–25; Luke 1:26–38). He took on Himself sinless human nature and identified with us in every aspect of life from birth to death. "The Word" was not an abstract concept of philosophy, but a real Person who could be seen, touched, and heard. Christianity is Christ, and Christ is God.

The revelation of God's glory is an important theme in the gospel. Jesus revealed God's glory in His person, His works, and His words. John recorded seven wonderful signs (miracles) that openly declared the glory of

God (John 2:11). The glory of the old covenant of law was a fading glory, but the glory of the new covenant in Christ is an increasing glory (see 2 Cor. 3). The law could reveal sin, but it could never remove sin. Jesus Christ came with *fullness* of grace and truth, and this fullness is available to all who will trust Him (John 1:16).

2. THE LIGHT (1:4–13)

Life is a key theme in John's gospel; it is used thirty-six times. What are the essentials for human life? There are at least four: light (if the sun went out, everything would die), air, water, and food. Jesus is all of these! He is the Light of Life and the Light of the World (John 8:12). He is the "Sun of righteousness" (Mal. 4:2). By His Holy Spirit, He gives us the "breath of life" (John 3:8; 20:22), as well as the Water of Life (John 4:10, 13–14; 7:37–39). Finally, Jesus is the Living Bread of Life that came down from heaven (John 6:35ff.). He not only has life and gives life, but He is life (John 14:6).

Light and darkness are recurring themes in John's gospel. God is light (1 John 1:5), while Satan is "the power of darkness" (Luke 22:53). People love either the light or the darkness, and this love controls their actions (John 3:16–19). Those who believe in Christ are the "sons of light" (John 12:35–36). Just as the first creation began with "Let there be light!" so the new creation begins with the entrance of light into the heart of the believer (2 Cor. 4:3–6). The coming of Jesus Christ into the world was the dawning of a new day for sinful humanity (Luke 1:78–79).

You would think that blind sinners would welcome the light, but such is not always the case. The coming of the true Light brought conflict as the powers of darkness opposed it. A literal translation of John 1:5 reads, "And the light keeps on shining in the darkness, and the darkness has not overcome it or understood it." The Greek verb can mean "to overcome" or "to grasp, to understand." Throughout the gospel of John, you will see both attitudes revealed: People will not understand what the Lord is saying and doing; and, as a result, they will oppose Him. John 7—12 records the growth of that opposition, which ultimately led to the crucifixion of Christ.

Whenever Jesus taught a spiritual truth, His listeners interpreted it in a material or physical way. The light was unable to penetrate the darkness in their minds. This was true when He spoke about the temple of His body (John 2:19–21), the new birth (John 3:4), the living water (John 4:11), eating His flesh (John 6:51ff.), spiritual freedom (John 8:30–36), death as sleep (John 11:11–13), and many other spiritual truths. Satan strives to keep people in the darkness, because darkness means death and hell, while light means life and heaven.

This fact helps explain the ministry of John the Baptist (John 1:6–8). John was sent as a witness to Jesus Christ, to tell people that the Light had come into the world. The nation of Israel, in spite of all its spiritual advantages, was blind to its own Messiah! The word *witness* is a key word in this book; John uses the noun fourteen times and the verb thirty-three times. John the Baptist was one of many people who bore witness to Jesus: "This is the Son of God!" Alas, John the Baptist was martyred, and the Jewish leaders did nothing to prevent it.

Why did the nation reject Jesus Christ? Because they "knew him not." They were spiritually ignorant. Jesus is the "true Light"—the original of which every other light is a copy—but the Jews were content with the copies. They had Moses and the law, the temple and the sacrifices, but they did not comprehend that these "lights" pointed to the true Light who was the fulfillment, the completion, of the Old Testament religion.

As you study John's gospel, you will find Jesus teaching the people that He is the fulfillment of all that was typified in the law. It was not enough to be born a Jew; they had to be born again, born from above (John 3). He deliberately performed two miracles on the Sabbath to teach them that He had a new rest to give them (John 5; 9). He was the satisfying manna (John 6) and the life-giving Water (John 7:37–39). He is the Shepherd of a new flock (John 10:16), and He is a new Vine (John 15). But the people were so shackled by religious tradition that they could not understand spiritual truth. Jesus came to His own world that He had created, but His own people, Israel, could not understand Him and would not receive Him.

They saw His works and heard His words. They observed His perfect life. He gave them every opportunity to grasp the truth, believe, and be saved. Jesus is the way, but they would not walk with Him (John 6:66–71). He is the truth, but they would not believe Him (John 12:37ff.). He is the life, and they crucified Him!

But sinners today need not commit those same blunders. John 1:12–13 gives us the marvelous promise of God that anyone who receives Christ will be born again and enter the family of God! John says more about this new birth in John 3, but he points out here that it is a spiritual birth from God, not a physical birth that depends on human nature.

The Light is still shining! Have you *personally* received the Light and become a child of God?

3. THE SON OF GOD (1:15–28, 49)

John the Baptist is one of the most important persons in the New Testament. He is mentioned at least eighty-nine times. John had the special privilege of introducing Jesus to the nation of Israel. He also had the difficult task of preparing the nation to receive its Messiah. He called them to repent of their sins and to prove that repentance by being baptized and then living changed lives.

John summarized what John the Baptist had to say about Jesus Christ (John 1:15–18). First, *He is eternal* (John 1:15). John the Baptist was actually born six months before Jesus (Luke 1:36), so in this statement he is referring to our Lord's preexistence, not His birth date. Jesus existed before John the Baptist was ever conceived.

Jesus Christ *has fullness of grace and truth* (John 1:16–17). Grace is God's favor and kindness bestowed on those who do not deserve it and cannot earn it. If God dealt with us only according to truth, none of us would survive, but He deals with us on the basis of grace *and* truth. Jesus Christ, in His life, death, and resurrection, met all the demands of the law; now God is free to share fullness of grace with those who trust Christ. Grace without truth would be deceitful, and truth without grace would be condemning.

In John 1:17, John did not suggest that there was no grace under the law of Moses, because there was. Each sacrifice was an expression of the grace of God. The law also revealed God's truth. But in Jesus Christ, grace and truth reach their fullness, and this fullness is available to us. We are saved by grace (Eph. 2:8–9), but we also live by grace (1 Cor. 15:10) and depend on God's grace in all that we do. We can receive one grace after another, for He "giveth more grace" (James 4:6). In John 1:17, John hinted that a whole new order had come in, replacing the Mosaic system.

Finally, *Jesus Christ reveals God to us* (John 1:18). As to His essence, God is invisible (1 Tim. 1:17; Heb. 11:27). People can see God revealed in nature (Ps. 19:1–6; Rom. 1:20) and in His mighty works in history, but they cannot see God Himself. Jesus Christ reveals God to us, for He is "the image of the invisible God" (Col. 1:15) and "the express image of his person" (Heb. 1:3). The word translated "declared" gives us our English word *exegesis,* which means "to explain, to unfold, to lead the way." Jesus Christ explains God to us and interprets Him for us. We simply cannot understand God apart from knowing His Son, Jesus Christ.

The word *Son* is used for the first time in John's gospel as a title for

Jesus Christ (John 1:18). The phrase "only begotten" means "unique, the only one of its kind." It does not suggest that there was a time when the Son was not and that then the Father brought Him into being. Jesus Christ is eternal God; He has always existed.

At least nine times in John's gospel, Jesus is called "the Son of God" (John 1:34, 49; 3:18; 5:25; 10:36; 11:4, 27; 19:7; 20:31). You will recall that John had as his purpose in writing to convince us that Jesus is the Son of God (John 20:31). At least nineteen times, Jesus is referred to as "the Son." He is not only the Son of God, but He is also God the Son. Even the demons admitted this (Mark 3:11; Luke 4:41).

John the Baptist is one of six persons named in the gospel of John who gave witness that Jesus is God. The others are Nathanael (John 1:49), Peter (John 6:69), the blind man who was healed (John 9:35–38), Martha (John 11:27), and Thomas (John 20:28). If you add our Lord Himself (John 5:25; 10:36), then you have seven clear witnesses.

John gave the record of four days in the life of John the Baptist, Jesus, and the first disciples. He continues this sequence in John 2 and presents, as it were, a "week" in the "new creation" that parallels the creation week in Genesis 1.

On the first day (John 1:19–24), a committee from the Jewish religious leaders interrogated John the Baptist. These men had every right to investigate John and his ministry, since they were the custodians and guardians of the faith. They asked him several questions, and he clearly answered them.

"Who are you?" was a logical question. Was he the promised Messiah? Was he the prophet Elijah who was supposed to come before the Messiah appeared (Mal. 4:5)? Great crowds had gathered to hear John, and many people had been baptized. Though John did no miracles (John 10:41), it was possible the people thought that he was the promised Messiah.

John denied being either Elijah or the Messiah. (In one sense, he was the promised Elijah. See Matt. 17:10–13.) John had nothing to say about himself because he was sent to talk about Jesus! Jesus is the Word; John was but "a voice"—and you cannot see a voice! John pointed back to Isaiah's prophecy (Isa. 40:1–3) and affirmed that he was the fulfillment.

Having ascertained who John was, the committee then asked what he was doing. "Why are you baptizing?" John got his authority to baptize, not from men, but from heaven, because he was commissioned by God (Matt. 21:23–32). The Jewish religious leaders in that day baptized Gentiles who wanted to adopt the Jewish faith, *but John baptized Jews!*

John explained that his baptism was in water, but that the Messiah would come and baptize with a spiritual baptism. Again, John made it clear that he was not establishing a new religion or seeking to exalt himself. He was pointing people to the Savior, the Son of God (John 1:34). We shall learn later that it was through baptism that Jesus Christ would be presented to the people of Israel.

4. LAMB OF GOD (1:29–34)

This is the second day of the week that the apostle John recorded, and no doubt some of the same committee members were present to hear John the Baptist's message. This time, he called Jesus "the Lamb of God," a title he would repeat the next day (John 1:35–36). In one sense, the message of the Bible can be summed up in this title. The question in the Old Testament is, "Where is the lamb?" (Gen. 22:7). In the four gospels, the emphasis is "Behold the Lamb of God!" Here He is! After you have trusted Him, you sing with the heavenly choir, "Worthy is the Lamb" (Rev. 5:12).

The people of Israel were familiar with lambs for the sacrifices. At Passover, each family had to have a lamb, and during the year, two lambs a day were sacrificed at the temple altar, plus all the other lambs brought for personal sacrifices. Those lambs were brought by people to people, but here is God's Lamb, given by God to humankind! Those lambs could not take away sin, but the Lamb of God can take away sin. Those lambs were for Israel alone, but this Lamb would shed His blood for the whole world!

What does John's baptism have to do with Jesus as the Lamb of God? It is generally agreed by scholars of all denominations that, in the New Testament, baptism was by immersion. It pictured death, burial, and resurrection. When John the Baptist baptized Jesus, Jesus and John were picturing the "baptism" Jesus would endure *on the cross* when He would die as the sacrificial Lamb of God (Isa. 53:7; Luke 12:50). It would be through death, burial, and resurrection that the Lamb of God would "fulfill all righteousness" (Matt. 3:15).

Perhaps John was mistaken. Perhaps John was not sure that Jesus of Nazareth was the Lamb of God or the Son of God. But the Father made it clear to John just who Jesus is by sending the Spirit like a dove to light on Him. What a beautiful picture of the Trinity!

5. The Messiah (1:35–42)

This is now the third day in the sequence. The seventh day included the wedding at Cana (John 2:1), and since Jewish weddings traditionally were on Wednesdays, it would make this third day the Sabbath day. But it was not a day of rest for either John the Baptist or Jesus, for John was preaching and Jesus was gathering disciples.

The two disciples of John who followed Jesus were John, the writer of the gospel, and his friend Andrew. John the Baptist was happy when people left him to follow Jesus, because his ministry focused on Jesus. "He must increase, but I must decrease" (John 3:30).

When Jesus asked them, "What are you seeking?" He was forcing them to define their purposes and goals. Were they looking for a revolutionary leader to overthrow Rome? Then they had better join the Zealots! Little did Andrew and John realize that day how their lives would be transformed by the Son of God.

"Where are You dwelling?" may have suggested, "If You are too busy now, we can visit later." But Jesus invited them to spend the day with Him (it was 10:00 a.m.); and no doubt He told them something of His mission, revealed their own hearts to them, and answered their questions. They were both so impressed that they found their brothers and brought them to Jesus. Andrew found Simon and John brought James. Indeed, they *were* their brothers' keepers (Gen. 4:9)! Whenever you find Andrew in John's gospel, he is bringing somebody to Jesus: his brother, the lad with the loaves and fish (John 6:8–9), and the Greeks who wanted to see Jesus (John 12:20–21). No sermons from Andrew are recorded, but he certainly preached great sermons by his actions as a personal soul winner!

"We have found the Messiah!" was the witness Andrew gave to Simon. *Messiah* is a Hebrew word that means "anointed," and the Greek equivalent is "Christ." To the Jews, it was the same as "Son of God" (see Matt. 26:63–64; Mark 14:61–62; Luke 22:67–70). In the Old Testament, prophets, priests, and kings were anointed and thereby set apart for special service. Kings were especially called "God's anointed" (1 Sam. 26:11; Ps. 89:20); so, when the Jews spoke about their Messiah, they were thinking of the king who would come to deliver them and establish the kingdom.

There was some confusion among the Jewish teachers as to what the Messiah would do. Some saw Him as a suffering sacrifice (as in Isa. 53), while others saw a splendid king (as in Isa. 9 and 11). Jesus had to explain even to His own followers that the cross had to come before the crown, that He must suffer before He could enter into His glory (Luke 24:13–35). Whether or not Jesus was indeed the Messiah was a crucial problem that challenged the Jews in that day (John 7:26, 40–44; 9:22; 10:24).

Simon's interview with Jesus changed his life. It also gave him a new name—*Peter* in the Greek, *Cephas* in the Aramaic that Jesus spoke, both of which mean "a rock." It took a great deal of work for Jesus to transform weak Simon into a rock, but He did it! "Thou art … thou shalt be" is a great encouragement to all who trust Christ. Truly, He gives us the "power to become" (John 1:12).

It is worth noting that Andrew and John trusted Christ through the faithful preaching of John the Baptist. Peter and James came to Christ because of the compassionate personal work of their brothers. Later on, Jesus would win Philip personally, and then Philip would witness to Nathanael and bring him to Jesus. Each person's experience is different, because God uses various means to bring sinners to the Savior. The important thing is that we trust Christ and then seek to bring others to Him.

6. THE KING OF ISRAEL (1:43–49)

Jesus called Philip personally, and Philip trusted Him and followed Him. We do not know what kind of heart preparation Philip experienced, for usually God prepares a person before He calls him. We do know that Philip proved his faith by seeking to share it with his friend Nathanael.

John 21:2 suggests that at least seven of our Lord's disciples were fishermen, including Nathanael. Fishermen are courageous and stick to the job, no matter how difficult it may be. But Nathanael started out a doubter; he did not believe that anything worthwhile could come out of Nazareth. Our Lord was born in Bethlehem, but He grew up in Nazareth and bore that stigma (Matt. 2:19–23). To be called "a Nazarene" (Acts 24:5) meant to be looked down on and rejected.

When Nathanael hesitated and argued, Philip adopted our Lord's own words: "Come and see" (John 1:39). Later on, Jesus would invite, "Come … and drink" (John 7:37), and, "Come and dine" (John 21:12). "Come" is the great invitation of God's grace.

When Nathanael came to Jesus, he discovered that the Lord already knew all about him! What a shock! By calling him "an Israelite in whom is no guile," Jesus was certainly referring to Jacob, the ancestor of the Jews, a man who used guile to trick his brother, his father, and his father-in-law. Jacob's name was changed to "Israel, a prince with God." The reference to "Jacob's ladder" in John 1:51 confirms this.

When Jesus revealed His knowledge of Nathanael, where he had been and what he had been doing, this was enough to convince the man that Jesus indeed was "the Son of God, the King of Israel." His experience was like that of the Samaritan woman at the well. "When he [Messiah] is come, he will tell us all things.... Come, see a man, which told me all things that ever I did" (John 4:25, 29). The revealing of the human heart should also take place in the ministry of local churches (1 Cor. 14:23–35).

When Philip witnessed to Nathanael, the evidence he gave was Moses and the prophets (John 1:45). Perhaps Jesus gave Philip a "quick course" in the Old Testament messianic prophecies, as He did with the Emmaus disciples (Luke 24:13ff.). It is always good to tie our personal witness to the Word of God.

"King of Israel" would be a title similar to "Messiah, Anointed One," for the kings were always God's anointed (see Ps. 2, especially vv. 2, 6–7). At one point in His ministry, the crowds wanted to make Jesus King, but He refused them (John 6:15ff.). He did present Himself as King (John 12:10ff.), and He affirmed to Pilate that He was born a King (John 18:33–37).

Some students believe that Nathanael and Bartholomew are the same person. John never mentions Bartholomew in his gospel, but the other three writers name Bartholomew and not Nathanael. Philip is linked with Bartholomew in the lists of names (Matt. 10:3; Mark 3:18; Luke 6:14), so it is possible that the two men were "paired off" and served together. It was not unusual in that day for one man to have two different names.

7. THE SON OF MAN (1:50–51)

"Son of man" was one of our Lord's favorite titles for Himself; it is used eighty-three times in the Gospels and at least thirteen times in John. The title speaks of both the deity and the humanity of Jesus. The vision in Daniel 7:13 presents the "Son of man" in a definite messianic setting, and Jesus used the title in the same way (Matt. 26:64).

As Son of Man, Jesus is the "living link" between heaven and earth. This explains His reference to "Jacob's ladder" in Genesis 28. Jacob the fugitive thought he was alone, but God had sent the angels to guard and guide him. Christ is God's "ladder" between heaven and earth. "No man cometh unto the Father, but by me" (John 14:6). Often in this gospel, you will find Jesus reminding people that He came down from heaven. The Jewish people knew that "Son of man" was a name for their Messiah (John 12:34).

At the close of that fourth day, Jesus had six believing men who were His disciples. They did not immediately "forsake all and follow him"; that was to come later. But they had trusted Him and experienced His power. In the three years that lay ahead, they would grow in their faith, learn more about Jesus, and one day take His place on the earth so that the Word might be carried to all humankind.

Jesus of Nazareth is God come in the flesh. When Philip called Him "the son of Joseph," he was not denying Jesus' virgin birth or divine nature. That was merely His legal identification, for a Jewish person was identified according to who his father was (John 6:42). The witness of this entire chapter is clear: Jesus of Nazareth is God come in the flesh!

God is here!

QUESTIONS FOR PERSONAL REFLECTION
OR GROUP DISCUSSION

1. How does the world portray Jesus today?

2. What does each of these names and titles that John used to describe Jesus tell us about Him: Word, Light, Son of God, Lamb of God, Messiah, King of Israel, Son of Man?

3. Choose one of these names or titles and describe how it is important for you personally.

4. Why was the Word made flesh?

5. What do you learn about John the Baptist and his relationship to Jesus in this first chapter?

6. By the end of His fourth day of ministry Jesus had six disciples. How did they come to believe in Him?

7. What do you learn about evangelism from the way they were made disciples?

8. What is the most significant thing you learned about Jesus from this chapter?

9. How can that significant thing influence the way you live this week?

Chapter Two

LEARNING ABOUT JESUS

(John 2)

The six disciples who now trusted Jesus started on their lifelong walk with Him and from the beginning began to learn more about Him. We who read the gospel record in its entirety are prone to take these events for granted, but to the disciples, each day and each new event brought marvels that were difficult to understand. In this chapter alone, John recorded three wonderful revelations of Jesus Christ.

1. HIS GLORY (2:1–12)

"The third day" means three days after the call of Nathanael (John 1:45–51). Since that was the fourth day of the week recorded in John (John 1:19, 29, 35, 43), the wedding took place on "the seventh day" of this "new creation week." Throughout his gospel, John makes it clear that Jesus was on a divine schedule, obeying the will of the Father.

Jewish tradition required that virgins be married on a Wednesday, while widows were married on a Thursday. Being the "seventh day" of John's special week, Jesus would be expected to rest, just as God rested on the seventh day (Gen. 2:1–3). But sin had interrupted God's Sabbath rest, and it was necessary for both the Father and the Son to work (John 5:17;

9:4). In fact, John recorded two specific miracles that Jesus deliberately performed on Sabbath days (John 5; 9).

At this wedding, we see Jesus in three different roles: the Guest, the Son, and the Host.

(1) Jesus the Guest (vv. 1–2). Our Lord was not a recluse, as was John the Baptist (Matt. 11:16–19). He accepted invitations to social events, even though His enemies used this practice to accuse Him (Luke 15:1–2). Our Lord entered into the normal experiences of life and sanctified them by His presence. Wise are the couple who invite Jesus to their wedding!

He was accompanied by His mother and His six disciples. Perhaps it was the addition of seven more people that helped create the crisis, but it must have been a small wedding feast if this were the case. We have reason to believe that our Lord's earthly family was not prosperous, and it is likely that their friends were not wealthy people. Perhaps the shortage of wine was related to a low-budget feast.

Were Jesus and His disciples invited because of Mary or because of Nathanael (John 21:2)? Our Lord was not yet well known; He had performed no miracles as yet. It was not likely that He was invited because the people knew who He was. It was probably His relationship with Mary that brought about the invitation.

(2) Jesus the Son (vv. 3–5). Since Jewish wedding feasts lasted a week, it was necessary for the groom to have adequate provisions. For one thing, it would be embarrassing to run out of either food or wine, and a family guilty of such gaucherie could actually be fined! So, to run out of wine could be costly both financially and socially.

Why did Mary approach Jesus about the problem? Did she actually expect Him to do something special to meet the need? Certainly she knew who He was, even though she did not declare this wonderful truth to others. She must have been very close to either the bride or the bridegroom to have such a personal concern for the success of the festivities or even to know that the supply of wine was depleted. Perhaps Mary was assisting in the preparation and serving of the meal.

Mary did not tell Jesus what to do; she simply reported the problem. (Compare the message of Mary and Martha to Jesus when Lazarus was sick—John 11:3.) Jesus' reply seems a bit abrupt and even harsh, but such is not the case. "Woman" was a polite way to address her (John 19:26; 20:13), and His statement merely means, "Why are you getting Me involved in this matter?" He was making it clear to His mother that He was no longer under her supervision (it is likely that Joseph was dead), but that from now on, He would be doing what the Father wanted Him to do. There had been a hint of this some years before (Luke 2:40–52).

At this point, John introduced one of the key elements of his record, the idea of "the hour." Jesus lived on a "heavenly timetable," marked out for Him by the Father. (See John 7:30; 8:20; 12:23; 13:1; 17:1; and note also the words of Jesus as recorded in John 11:9–10.) As you study John's gospel, you will observe how this concept of "the hour" is developed.

Mary's words to the servants reveal that she was willing to let her Son do whatever He pleased and that she trusted Him to do what was right. It would be wise for all of us to obey what she said! It is worth noting that it was Jesus, not Mary, who took command and solved the problem; and that Mary pointed, not to herself, but to Jesus.

(3) Jesus the Host (vv. 6–12). Our Lord's first miracle was not a spectacular event that everybody witnessed. Mary, the disciples, and the servants knew what had happened; but nobody else at the feast had any idea that a miracle had taken place. His first miracle was a quiet event at a wedding in contrast to His last miracle recorded by John (John 11), a public event after a funeral.

Each of the six stone waterpots could contain about twenty gallons each. However, we are not told that all of the available water in the jars turned into wine. Only that which the servants drew out and served was transformed into wine. The quality of this new wine was so superior that the man in charge of the banquet highly praised it, and, of course, the groom's family basked in the glory of the compliments.

The fact that this was the "beginning of miracles" automatically declares as false the stories about the miracles performed by Jesus when He was an infant or a young child. They are nothing but superstitious fables and ought to be rejected by anyone who accepts the authority of the Bible.

The miracle did something for His disciples. It revealed His glory (John 1:14) and gave them a stronger foundation for their faith. Though miracles *alone* are insufficient evidence for declaring Jesus to be the Son of God (2 Thess. 2:9–10), the cumulative effect of miracle after miracle should certainly convince them of His deity. The disciples had to begin somewhere, and over the months, their faith deepened as they got to know Jesus better.

But there is certainly more to this miracle than simply meeting a human need and saving a family from social embarrassment. The gospel of John, unlike the other three gospels, seeks to share the *inner meaning*— the spiritual significance—of our Lord's works, so that each miracle is a "sermon in action." We must be careful not to "spiritualize" these events so that they lose their historical moorings, but, at the same time, we must not be so shackled to history that we are blind to (as A. T. Pierson used to say) "His story."

To begin with, the word John used in his book is not *dunamis,* which emphasizes power, but *sīmeion,* which means "a sign." What is a sign? Something that points beyond itself to something greater. It was not enough for people to believe in Jesus' works; they had to believe in Him and in the Father who sent Him (John 5:14–24). This explains why Jesus often added a sermon to the miracle and in that sermon interpreted the sign. In John 5, the healing of the paralytic on the Sabbath opened the way for a message on His deity, "the Lord of the Sabbath." The feeding of the five thousand (John 6) led naturally into a sermon on the Bread of Life.

If our Lord had preached a sermon after He turned the water into wine, what might He have said? For one thing, He likely would have told the people that the world's joy always runs out and cannot be regained, but the joy He gives is ever new and ever satisfying. (In the Scriptures, wine is a symbol of joy. See Judg. 9:13; Ps. 104:15.) The world offers the best at the first; and then, once you are "hooked," things start to get worse. But Jesus continues to offer that which is best until we one day enjoy the finest blessings in the eternal kingdom (Luke 22:18).

But our Lord would certainly have a special message here for His people, Israel. In the Old Testament, the nation is pictured as "married" to God and unfaithful to her marriage covenant (Isa. 54:5; Jer. 31:32; Hos. 2:2ff.). The wine ran out, and all Israel had left were six empty waterpots! They held water for *external* washings, but they could provide nothing for internal cleaning and joy. In this miracle, our Lord brought fullness where there was emptiness, joy where there was disappointment, and something *internal* for that which was only external (water for ceremonial washings).

When John mentioned "the third day" (John 2:1), he may have been giving us a hint of our Lord's resurrection. All of these blessings are possible because of His sacrifice on the cross and His resurrection from the dead (John 2:19).

Interestingly Moses' first miracle was a plague—turning water into blood (Ex. 7:19ff.), which speaks of judgment. Our Lord's first miracle spoke of grace.

This miracle also presents a practical lesson in service for God. The water turned into wine because the servants cooperated with Jesus and obeyed His commands. Several of the signs in John's gospel involve the cooperation of people and God: the feeding of the five thousand (John 6), the healing of the man born blind (John 9), and the raising of Lazarus (John 11). Whether we pass out bread, wash away mud, or roll away the stone, we are assisting Him in performing a miracle.

It is significant that the servants knew the source of this special wine (John 2:9). When Jesus healed the nobleman's son (John 4:46–54), it was the servants who were in on the secret. We are not just His servants; we are also His friends, and we know what He is doing (John 15:15).

Wine was the normal drink of the people in that day, and we must not use this miracle as an argument for the use of alcoholic beverages today. A man given to drink once said to me, "After all, Jesus turned water into wine!"

My reply was, "If you use Jesus as your example for drinking, why don't you follow His example in everything else?" Then I read Luke 22:18 to him. This verse clearly states that, in heaven now, Jesus is a teetotaler!

Sincere Christians of our day consider such verses as 1 Corinthians 8:9; 10:23, 31 before concluding that the use of alcoholic beverages is a wise thing today. I am reminded of the story of the drunken coal miner who was converted and became a vocal witness for Christ. One of his friends tried to trap him by asking, "Do you believe that Jesus turned water into wine?"

"I certainly do!" the believer replied. "In my home, He has turned wine into furniture, decent clothes, and food for my children!"

Finally, it is worth noting that the Jews always diluted the wine with water, usually to the proportion of three parts water to one part wine.

While the Bible does not command total abstinence, it certainly *magnifies* it and definitely warns against drunkenness.

2. HIS ZEAL (2:12–22)

Jesus, His family, and His disciples remained in Capernaum a few days, and then He went to Jerusalem for the Passover Feast. Each Jewish man was required to attend three annual feasts at the Holy City: Passover, Pentecost, and Tabernacles (Deut. 16:16). The feasts mentioned in the gospel of John are Passover (John 2:13; 6:4; 12:1), Tabernacles (John 7:2), and Dedication (John 10:22). The unnamed feast in John 5:1 may have been Purim (Est. 9:26, 31).

Though He deliberately violated the man-made religious traditions of the Pharisees, our Lord obeyed the statutes of the law and was faithful to uphold the law. In His life and death, He fulfilled the law so that, today, believers are not burdened by that "yoke of bondage" (Acts 15:10).

Jesus revealed His zeal for God first of all by *cleansing the temple* (John 2:13–17). The priests had established a lucrative business of exchanging foreign money for Jewish currency and also selling the animals needed for the sacrifices. No doubt, this "religious market" began as a convenience for the Jews who came long distances to worship in the temple, but in due time the "convenience" became a business, not a ministry. The tragedy is that this business was carried on in the court of the Gentiles in the temple, the place where the Jews should have been meeting the Gentiles and telling them about the one true God. Any Gentile searching for truth would not likely find it among the religious merchants in the temple.

Our Lord suddenly appeared in the temple and cleaned house! He was careful not to destroy anyone's property (He did not release the doves, for example), but He made it clear that He was in command. The temple was His Father's house, and He would not have the religious leaders pollute it with their money-making enterprises.

The condition of the temple was a vivid indication of the spiritual condition of the nation. Their religion was a dull routine, presided over by worldly minded men whose main desire was to exercise authority and get rich. Not only had the wine run out at the wedding feast but the glory had departed from the temple.

When they saw His courageous zeal, the disciples remembered Psalm 69:9 "The zeal of [for] thine house hath eaten me up." Psalm 69 is definitely a messianic psalm that is quoted several times in the New Testament: Psalm 69:4 (John 15:25); Psalm 69:8 (John 7:3–5); Psalm 69:9 (John 2:17; Rom. 15:3); Psalm 69:21 (Matt. 27:34, 48); and Psalm 69:22 (Rom. 11:9–10).

There was still a godly remnant in Israel who loved God and revered His temple (Luke 1:5–22; 2:25–38), but most religious leaders were false shepherds who exploited the people. When Jesus cleansed the temple, He "declared war" on the hypocritical religious leaders (Matt. 23), and this ultimately led to His death. Indeed, His zeal for God's house *did* eat Him up!

He also revealed His zeal by *giving His life* (John 2:18–22). It was logical for the religious leaders to ask Him to show the source of His authority. After all, they were the guardians of the Jewish faith, and they had a right to test any new prophet who appeared. "The Jews require a sign" (1 Cor. 1:22). Often, during His ministry, the leaders asked Jesus to give them a sign, and He refused to do so, *except* for the sign of Jonah (Matt. 12:39ff.). The "sign of Jonah" is death, burial, and resurrection.

Jesus used the image of the temple to convey this truth. "Destroy this temple [My body], and in three days I will raise it up" (John 2:19). Being spiritually blind, those who heard misunderstood what He was saying.

Throughout the gospel of John, you will find people misunderstanding *spiritual* truth and interpreting in material or physical terms (John 3:4; 4:11; 6:52). Herod's temple was started in 20 BC and not completed until AD 64. How could one man "raise it up" in three days?

This statement was, of course, a prediction of His own death and resurrection, and His disciples remembered it after He was raised from the dead. But His enemies also remembered it and used it at His trial (Matt. 26:59–61), and some of the people mocked Him with it when He was dying on the cross (Matt. 27:40).

In writing this gospel, John included a number of vivid pictures of the death of the Savior. The first is the slaying of the Lamb in John 1:29, indicating that His death would be that of a substitute for sinners. The destroying of the temple is the second picture (John 2:19), suggesting a violent death that would end in victorious resurrection.

The third picture is that of the serpent lifted up (John 3:14), a reference to Numbers 21:5–9. The Savior would be made sin for us (1 Peter 2:24). His death would be voluntary (John 10:11–18): The Shepherd would lay down His life for the sheep. Finally, the planting of the seed (John 12:20–25) teaches that His death would produce fruit to the glory of God. His death and burial would look like failure, but in the end, God would bring victory.

The temple was an important element of the Jewish faith, for in it God was supposed to dwell. All of the ceremonies and sacrifices of the Jewish religion centered in the temple. When Jesus suggested that their precious building would be destroyed, their angry reaction was predictable. After all, if *His* body is the temple, then the Jewish temple would be needed no more. In this cryptic statement, our Lord actually predicted the end of the Jewish religious system.

But that was one of the purposes John had in mind when he wrote his gospel: The legal system has ended, and "grace and truth" have come through Jesus Christ. He is the new sacrifice (John 1:29) and the new temple (John 2:19). John will tell us later that the new worship will depend on inward integrity, not outward geography (John 4:19–24).

3. HIS KNOWLEDGE (2:23–25)

While in Jerusalem for the Passover, Jesus performed miracles that are not given in detail in any of the Gospels. It must have been these signs that especially attracted Nicodemus (John 3:2). Because of the miracles, many people professed to believe in Him, but Jesus did not accept their profession. No matter what the people themselves said or others said about them. He did not accept human testimony. Why? Because, being God, He knew what was in each person's heart and mind.

The words *believed* in John 2:23 and *commit* in John 2:24 are the same Greek word. These people believed in Jesus, but He did not believe in them! They were "unsaved believers"! It was one thing to respond to a miracle but quite something else to commit oneself to Jesus Christ and continue in His Word (John 8:30–31).

John was not discrediting the importance of our Lord's signs, because he wrote his book to record these signs and to encourage his readers to trust Jesus Christ and receive eternal life (John 20:30–31). However, throughout the book, John makes it clear that it takes more than believing in miracles for a person to be saved. Seeing the signs and believing in them would be a great beginning; in fact, even the disciples started that way and had to grow in their faith (compare John 2:11 and 22).

Throughout the gospel of John, you see the Jewish people divided over the meaning of these miracles (John 9:16; 11:45–46). The same miracles that attracted Nicodemus to Jesus caused some of the other religious leaders to want to kill Him! They even asserted that His miracles were done in the power of Satan! Our Lord's miracles were testimonies (John 5:36), giving evidence of His divine sonship; but they were also *tests,* exposing the hearts of the people (John 12:37ff.). The same events that opened some eyes only made other eyes that much more blind (John 9:39–41).

It is important to see that Jesus tied His miracles to the truth of His message. He knew that the human heart is attracted to the sensational. The five thousand who He fed wanted to make Him King—until He preached a sermon on the Bread of Life, and then they left Him in droves! "Grace and truth came by Jesus Christ" (John 1:17). In grace, Jesus fed the hungry; in truth, He taught the Word. The people wanted the physical food but not the spiritual truth, so they abandoned Him.

"He knew what was in man" is a statement that is proved several times in John's gospel. Jesus knew the character of Simon (John 1:42). He knew what Nathanael was like (John 1:46ff.), and He told the Samaritan woman "all things" that she had ever done (John 4:29). He knew that the Jewish leaders did not have God's love in their hearts (John 5:42) and that one of His disciples was not truly a believer (John 6:64). He saw the repentance in the heart of the adulteress (John 8:10–11) and the murder in the hearts of His enemies (John 8:40ff.). Several times in the upper room message, Jesus revealed to His disciples their own inner feelings and questions.

As you follow our Lord's ministry in John's gospel, you see Him moving gradually out of the bright light of popularity and into the dark shadows of rejection. At the beginning, it was easy for people to follow the crowd and watch His miracles. But then, His words began to penetrate hearts, with conviction following, and conviction leads either to conversion or opposition. It is impossible to be neutral. People had to decide, and most of them decided against Him.

Yes, Jesus knows the human heart. "Except ye see signs and wonders, ye will not believe" (John 4:48). People who want His works but not His

Word can never share His life. "Seeing is believing" is not the Christian approach (John 11:40; 20:29). First we believe; then we see. Miracles can only lead us to the Word (John 5:36–38), and the Word generates saving faith (Rom. 10:17).

Our Lord's accurate knowledge of the human heart is another evidence of His deity, for only God can see the inner person. This brief paragraph prepares us for the important interview with Nicodemus recorded in the next chapter. Note the repetition of the word *man* from John 2:25 to 3:1. Nicodemus wanted to learn more about Jesus, but he ended up learning more about himself!

QUESTIONS FOR PERSONAL REFLECTION
OR GROUP DISCUSSION

1. When you first came to know Jesus, which of His characteristics had the deepest influence on you?

2. Skim through this chapter. If you were one of Jesus disciples, what would you think of Him? Why?

3. Read John 2:1–12. What does it say about Jesus that He performed His first miracle at a wedding?

4. What impression of Mary does this story give you?

5. Jesus was on a schedule when He was here on earth. Why does that matter to us? What is the significance of the word *hour* in verse 4?

6. Turning the water into wine was the first of seven signs John recorded in this book. What did this sign point to?

7. Read verses 13–22. Why was Jesus so upset with those selling merchandise in the temple courts?

8. What is "zeal"? How is it different from fanaticism?

9. What statement was Jesus making with His actions in the temple courts?

10. Read verses 23–25. Why did John mention Jesus' knowledge?

11. How can Jesus' glory, zeal, and knowledge affect the way you live this week?

Chapter Three

A Matter of Life and Death

(John 3)

Not only was Benjamin Franklin a great statesman and inventor, but he was also a great correspondent and received letters from famous people from all over the world. One day he received what could well have been the most important letter ever to come to his desk. It was from the well-known British preacher George Whitefield.

"I find that you grow more and more famous in the learned world," Whitefield wrote. "As you have made such progress in investigating the mysteries of electricity, I now humbly urge you to give diligent heed to the mystery of the new birth. It is a most important and interesting study and, when mastered, will richly repay you for your pains."

The new birth is one of the key topics in John 3. In addition, in this chapter we see Jesus Christ in three different roles: the Teacher (John 3:1–21), the Bridegroom (John 3:22–30), and the Witness (John 3:31–36).

1. JESUS CHRIST THE TEACHER (3:1–21)

We have already noted the connection between John 2:23–25 and 3:1. Nicodemus was initially attracted to Jesus because of the miracles He did. He wanted to know more about Jesus and the doctrines that He taught.

Nicodemus himself was *"the* teacher of the Jews" (John 3:10, literal transla-tion), and he had great respect for the Teacher from Galilee.

Nicodemus was a Pharisee, which meant he lived by the strictest possible religious rules. Not all of the Pharisees were hypocrites (as one may infer from Jesus' comments recorded in Matt. 23), and evidence indicates that Nico-demus was deeply sincere in his quest for truth. He came to Jesus by night, not because he was afraid of being seen, but most likely because he wanted to have a quiet, uninterrupted conversation with the new Teacher "come from God." The fact that Nicodemus used the plural pronoun "we" and that Jesus responded with the plural "ye" (John 3:7) may indicate that Nicodemus was representing the religious leaders. He was a man of high moral character, deep religious hunger, and yet profound spiritual blindness.

In order to instruct Nicodemus in the basics of salvation, our Lord used four quite different illustrations.

(1) Birth (vv. 1–7). Our Lord began with that which was familiar, birth being a universal experience. The word translated "again" also means "from above." Though all human beings have experienced natural birth on earth, if they expect to go to heaven, they must experience a supernatural spiritual birth from above.

Once again, we meet with the blindness of sinners: This well-educated religious leader, Nicodemus, did not understand what the Savior was talking about! Jesus was speaking about a spiritual birth, but Nicodemus thought only of a physical birth. The situation is no different today. When you talk with people about being born again, they often begin to discuss their family's religious heritage, their church membership, their religious ceremonies, and so on.

Being a patient teacher, our Lord picked up on Nicodemus's words and further explained the new birth. To be "born of water" is to be born physi-cally ("enter a second time into his mother's womb"), but to be born again means to be born of the Spirit. Just as there are two parents for physical birth, so there are two "parents" for spiritual birth: the Spirit of God (John 3:5) and the Word of God (James 1:18; 1 Peter 1:23–25). The Spirit of God takes the Word of God and, when the sinner believes, imparts the life of God.

Jesus was not teaching that the new birth comes through water baptism. In the New Testament, baptism is connected with *death*, not birth, and no amount of physical water can effect a spiritual change in a person. The emphasis in John 3:14–21 is on *believing*, because salvation comes through faith (Eph. 2:8–9). The evidence of salvation is the witness of the Spirit within (Rom. 8:9), and the Spirit enters your life when you believe (Acts 10:43–48; Eph. 1:13–14).

Water baptism is certainly a part of our obedience to Christ and our witness for Christ (Matt. 28:18–20; Acts 2:41). But it must not be made an essential for salvation; otherwise, none of the Old Testament saints was ever saved, nor was the thief on the cross (Luke 23:39–43). In every age, there has been but one way of salvation—faith in God's promise—though the *outward evidence* of that faith has changed from age to age.

Human birth involves travail (John 16:21), and so does the birth from above. Our Savior had to travail on the cross so that we might become members of the family of God (Isa. 53:11). Concerned believers have to travail in prayer and witness as they seek to lead sinners to Christ (1 Cor. 4:15; Gal. 4:19).

The child inherits the nature of the parents, and so does the child of God. We become "partakers of the divine nature" (2 Peter 1:4). Nature determines appetite, which explains why the Christian has an appetite for the things of God (1 Peter 2:2–3). He has no desire to go back to the foul things of the world that once appealed to him (2 Peter 2:20–22). He feeds on the Word of God and grows into spiritual maturity (Heb. 5:11–14).

Of course, birth involves life, and spiritual birth from above involves

God's life. John uses the word *life* thirty-six times in his gospel. The opposite of life is death, and the person who has not believed on Jesus Christ does not have God's life, eternal life, abundant life. *You do not manufacture Christians any more than you manufacture babies!* The only way to enter God's family is through the new birth (John 1:11–13).

Birth involves a future, and we are "born again to a living hope" (1 Peter 1:3 NASB). A newborn baby cannot be arrested because he or she has no past! When you are born again into God's family, your sins are forgiven and forgotten, and your future is bright with a living hope.

Nicodemus must have had a surprised and yet bewildered look on his face, for the Lord had to say, "You must not be surprised that I told you that all of you must be born again" (John 3:7 PH). But Nicodemus was born a Jew! He was a part of God's covenant people (Rom. 9:4–5)! Certainly his birth was better than that of a Gentile or a Samaritan! And his life was exemplary, for he was a faithful Pharisee! He could well understand Jesus telling the *Romans* that they had to be born again, but certainly not the *Jews!*

(2) The wind (vv. 8–13). It is likely that the evening wind was blowing just then as Nicodemus and Jesus sat on the housetop, conversing. The word *wind* in both Hebrew and Greek can also be translated "spirit." One of the symbols of the Spirit of God in the Bible is the wind or breath (Job 33:4; John 20:22; Acts 2:2). Like the wind, the Spirit is invisible but powerful, and you cannot explain or predict the movements of the wind.

When Jesus used this symbol, Nicodemus should have readily remembered Ezekiel 37:1–14. The prophet saw a valley full of dead bones, but when he prophesied to the wind, the Spirit came and gave the bones life. Again, it was the combination of the Spirit of God and the Word of God that gave life. The nation of Israel (including Nicodemus and his fellow council members) was dead and hopeless, but in spite of the morality and religion of the people, they needed the life of the Spirit.

The new birth from above is a necessity ("Ye must be born again"), but it is also a mystery. Everyone who is born of the Spirit is like the wind: You cannot fully explain or predict either the wind or the child of God! For that matter, human birth is still a mystery, in spite of all that we know about anatomy and physiology. Each new life is exciting and different.

Nicodemus came "by night," and he was still in the dark! He could not understand the new birth even after Jesus had explained it to him. Our Lord stated clearly that Nicodemus's knowledge of the Old Testament should have given him the light he needed (John 3:10). Alas, "the teacher of the Jews" knew the *facts* recorded in the Scriptures, but he could not understand the *truths*.

What was the problem? For one thing, the religious leaders would not submit to the authority of Christ's witness (John 3:11). We will see this "authority conflict" increase as we continue in our studies. The religious leaders claimed to believe Moses, yet they could not believe Jesus (John 5:37–47). The Pharisees were more concerned about the praise of men than the praise of God (John 12:37–50).

"I have used earthly illustrations," said Jesus, "and you cannot understand. If I began to share the deep spiritual truths, you still would not believe" (see John 3:12).

(3) The serpent on the pole (vv. 14–18). The story in Numbers 21:4–9 was certainly familiar to Nicodemus. It is a story of sin, for the nation rebelled against God and had to be punished. God sent fiery serpents that bit the people so that many died. It is also a story of grace, for Moses interceded for the people, and God provided a remedy. He told Moses to make a brass serpent and lift it up on a pole for all to see. Any stricken person who looked at the serpent would immediately be healed. So, it is also a story of faith: When the people looked by faith, they were saved.

The verb *lifted up* has a dual meaning: to be crucified (John 8:28;

12:32–34) and to be glorified and exalted. In his gospel, John points out that our Lord's crucifixion was actually the means of His glorification (John 12:23ff.). The cross was not the end of His glory; it was the means of His glory (Acts 2:33).

Much as the serpent was lifted up on that pole, so the Son of God would be lifted up on a cross. Why? To save us from sin and death. In the camp of Israel, the solution to the "serpent problem" was not in killing the serpents, making medicine, pretending they were not there, passing antiserpent laws, or climbing the pole. The answer was in looking by faith at the uplifted serpent.

The whole world has been bitten by sin, and "the wages of sin is death" (Rom. 6:23). God sent His Son to die, not only for Israel, but for a whole world. How is a person born from above? How is he or she saved from eternal perishing? By believing on Jesus Christ; by looking to Him in faith.

On January 6, 1850, a snowstorm almost crippled the city of Colchester, England, and a teenage boy was unable to get to the church he usually attended. So he made his way to a nearby Primitive Methodist chapel, where an ill-prepared layman was substituting for the absent preacher. His text was Isaiah 45:22—"Look unto me, and be ye saved, all the ends of the earth." For many months this young teenager had been miserable and under deep conviction, but though he had been reared in church (both his father and grandfather were preachers), he did not have the assurance of salvation.

The unprepared substitute minister did not have much to say, so he kept repeating the text. "A man need not go to college to learn to look," he shouted. "Anyone can look—a child can look!" About that time, he saw the visitor sitting to one side, and he pointed at him and said, "Young man, you look very miserable. Young man, look to Jesus Christ!"

The young man did look by faith, and that was how the great preacher Charles Haddon Spurgeon was converted.

The difference between perishing and living, and between condemnation and salvation, is faith in Jesus Christ. Jesus could well have come to this world as a judge and destroyed every rebellious sinner; but in love, He came to this world as our Savior, *and He died for us on the cross!* He became the "uplifted serpent." The serpent in Moses' day brought physical life to dying Jews, but Jesus Christ gives eternal life to anyone who trusts Him. He has salvation for a whole world!

(4) **Light and darkness (vv. 19–21).** This is one of the major images used in this gospel (John 1:4–13). Why will sinners not come into the "light of life"? Because they love the darkness! They want to persist in their evil deeds, and this keeps them from coming to the light, for the closer the sinner gets to the light, the more his sins are exposed. It is not "intellectual problems" that keep people from trusting Christ; it is the moral and spiritual blindness that keeps them loving the darkness and hating the light.

Please note that Nicodemus finally did "come to the light." He was in the "midnight of confusion" (John 3:1–21), but eventually he came out into the "sunlight of confession" when he identified with Christ at Calvary (John 19:38–42). He realized that the uplifted Savior was indeed the Son of God.

2. Jesus the Bridegroom (3:22–30)

Until John the Baptist was arrested by Herod and put into prison, his ministry overlapped that of the Lord Jesus. John did not want anyone to follow him; his ministry was to point to the Lamb of God and urge people to trust Him. But when two popular preachers are involved in similar work, it is easy for both friends and enemies to get caught up in competition and comparison.

It appears that some of John's disciples started the argument. It began on doctrinal grounds—the matter of purifying—but soon moved to personal grounds. In John 3:25, some manuscripts read "a Jew" instead of "the

Jews." Could this unnamed Jew have possibly been Nicodemus? We cannot say, but it is a possibility.

The matter of purifying was important to the Jews (Mark 7:1–23). Under the Old Testament law, it was necessary for them to keep themselves ceremonially clean if they were to serve God and please Him. Unfortunately, the Pharisees added so many extra traditions to the law that the observing of it became a burden.

Without realizing it, John's disciples were putting him into a situation of competing against the Lord Jesus! "All men come to him." (John 3:26) sounds like a wail of despair. It is interesting to note that four of the greatest men in the Bible faced this problem of comparison and competition: Moses (Num. 11:26–30), John the Baptist (John 3:26–30), Jesus (Luke 9:46–50), and Paul (Phil. 1:15–18). A leader often suffers more from his zealous disciples than from his critics!

How did John the Baptist handle this controversy? To begin with, he stated a conviction: All ministry and blessing come from God, so there can be no competition (John 3:27). Paul would have agreed with this (1 Cor. 3:1–9; 4:1–7). Our gifts and opportunities come from God, and He alone must get the glory.

Then John used a beautiful illustration. He compared Jesus to the bridegroom and himself only to the best man (John 3:29). Once the bridegroom and bride had been brought together, the work of the best man was completed. What a foolish thing it would be for the best man to try to "upstage" the bridegroom and take his place. John's joy was to hear the voice of the Bridegroom and know that He had claimed His bride.

Even before his birth, John the Baptist rejoiced in the Lord (Luke 1:44). John was content to be the voice announcing Jesus to be the Word (John 1:23). Jesus was the Light, and John the Baptist was the witness pointing to the Light (John 1:6–8).

Often press releases and book reviews cross my desk, along with conference folders, and at times I am perturbed by what I read. Very few speakers and writers are ordinary people. They are "world travelers" or "noted lecturers" who have addressed "huge audiences." They are always in "great demand," and their ministries are described in such ways that they make the apostle Paul a midget by comparison.

A Presbyterian pastor in Melbourne, Australia, introduced J. Hudson Taylor by using many superlatives, especially the word *great*. Taylor stepped to the pulpit and quietly said, "Dear friends, I am the little servant of an illustrious Master." If John the Baptist in heaven heard that statement, he must have shouted, "Hallelujah!"

The image of the Bridegroom would have been significant to the Jewish people, for Jehovah had a "marriage covenant" with the nation (Isa. 54:5; 62:4ff.; Jer. 2:2; 3:20; Ezek. 16:8; Hos. 2:19ff.). Alas, Israel had been unfaithful to her vows, and God had to put her away temporarily. Today, God is calling out a people for His name, the church, the bride of Christ (2 Cor. 11:1–3; Eph. 5:22–33). One day the Bridegroom will come to claim His bride and take her to her home in heaven (Rev. 19:6–9; 21:9ff.).

The word *must* is used in three significant ways in this chapter: the "must" of the sinner (John 3:7), the "must" of the Savior (John 3:14), and the "must" of the servant (John 3:30).

3. Jesus the Witness (3:31–36)

Bible scholars do not agree as to who is speaking in John 3:31–36, John the apostle or John the Baptist. For that matter, some students believe that John 3:16–21 came from the apostle John and not the Lord Jesus. There were no quotation marks in early manuscripts, but since all Scripture is inspired, it really makes little difference who said the words.

The emphasis in this paragraph is on witness ("testimony"), one of the key subjects in John's gospel. The Greek word translated "witness" or "testimony" is used forty-seven times. John bore witness to Jesus (John 1:7; 5:33), but Jesus was also a witness to the truth. Why should we heed His witness? For several reasons.

He came from heaven (v. 31). He was not simply called from heaven or empowered by heaven; He *came* from heaven. It was this claim that the Jews disputed, because they knew it was His claim that He was God (John 6:38–42). John the Baptist certainly was not "from above," nor did he claim to be. No earthly messenger of God came "from above." Only Jesus Christ can make that claim and prove it to be true.

Since Jesus came from heaven, He represents the Father; and to reject His witness is to reject the Father (John 5:23). We know that His witness is true because He is the true God. We can trust it and rely on it.

It comes from Him firsthand (vv. 32–33). He shares what He has seen and heard from the Father (John 8:38). Those who receive His witness *and act on it* know by personal experience that His witness is true (John 7:17). Our Lord's teachings are not to be studied intellectually, separated from everyday life. It is when we obey His Word and put it into practice that we see its truth and experience its power.

The Father has authorized His Son (vv. 34–35). God sent Him (another key theme in John's gospel); God gave Him the Word; God gave Him the Spirit; and God gave Him all things (John 13:3). What a commissioning! To reject the Son's witness is to rebel against the highest authority in the universe.

We usually think of God's love for a lost world (John 3:16), but John reminds us of the Father's love for His Son. Jesus is the Father's "beloved Son" (Matt. 3:17; Mark 1:11; Luke 3:22). Because the Father loves the

Son, He has given Him all things, and He shows Him all things (John 5:20). It is a love that can hold nothing back.

Therefore, when we receive His witness, we share in His love and His wealth. To reject Christ's witness is to sin against love and light. No wonder our Lord wept over the city of Jerusalem (Matt. 23:37–39). They had rejected His witness—both His messages and His miracles—and their rejection led to judgment.

We might escape the wrath of God (v. 36). This is the only place in any of John's epistles or his gospel that he uses the word *wrath*. (He uses it six times in the book of Revelation.) This verse parallels John 3:18 and makes it clear that there can be no neutrality when it comes to the witness of Jesus Christ: Either we trust Him or we reject Him.

"Everlasting life" does not simply mean eternity in heaven. The believer possesses that life right now! It is the life of God in the believer. The opposite of eternal life is eternal death, the wrath of God. A person does not have to die and go to hell to be under the wrath of God. "He that believeth not is condemned already" (John 3:18). The verdict has already been given, but the sentence has not yet been executed. Why? Because God is patient and long suffering and continues to call sinners to repentance (2 Peter 3:9).

As you review John 3, you can see that the apostle John is emphasizing a personal relationship with Jesus Christ.

It is a *living relationship* that begins with the new birth, the birth from above. When we receive Jesus Christ into our lives, we share His very life and become children in the family of God.

It is also a *loving relationship,* for He is the Bridegroom, and we are a part of the bride. Like John the Baptist, we desire that Jesus Christ increase as we decrease. He must receive all the honor and glory.

It is a *learning relationship,* for He is the faithful Witness who shares

God's truth with us. What a delight it is to receive His Word, meditate on it, and make it part of our very lives.

But we must never forget the cost of these blessings. For us to be born into God's family, Jesus Christ had to die. For us to enter into the loving relationship of salvation, He had to endure the hatred and condemnation of humankind. He had to be lifted up on the cross so that we might experience forgiveness and eternal life.

May we never take this for granted!

"He must increase, but I must decrease" (John 3:30).

QUESTIONS FOR PERSONAL REFLECTION OR GROUP DISCUSSION

1. In what does the world try to find salvation today?

2. Read verses 1–21. What is your impression of Nicodemus?

3. Why did Jesus treat Nicodemus like a religious illiterate?

4. What does Jesus' self-confidence with another great rabbi suggest about His understanding of who He was?

5. Jesus used four illustrations to explain salvation to Nicodemus: birth, wind, the serpent on a pole, light, and darkness. What does each illustration contribute to your understanding of salvation?

6. Which of these illustrations is most helpful to you? Why?

7. Which illustration, if any of them, is hard for you to grasp? Why?

8. Read Numbers 21:4–9. Why did Jesus choose this illustration to teach Nicodemus more about salvation?

9. Read verses 22–30. Does it surprise you that John the Baptist wasn't concerned about his status as a religious leader? Why or why not?

10. How can we let Jesus increase while we decrease as John the Baptist did?

11. Read verses 31–36. Why should we heed Jesus' witness to the truth?

12. In this chapter, John emphasized that a personal relationship with Jesus is a living, loving, and learning one. How fully are you experiencing this relationship? What could help you?

Chapter Four

THE BAD SAMARITAN
(John 4)

In John 4, our Lord ministers to a variety of people: the sinful Samaritan woman, His own disciples, the many Samaritans who trusted in Him, and, finally, a nobleman and his household. What did these have in common? *Faith* in Jesus Christ. John was fulfilling the purpose of his gospel in showing his readers how various kinds and classes of people came to believe in Jesus as the Son of God.

Let's meet these various persons and discover how their faith began, how it grew, and what it did for them and for others.

THE SAMARITAN WOMAN (4:1–30)

Because the Pharisees were trying to incite competition between Jesus and John the Baptist (John 3:25–30), Jesus left Judea and started north for Galilee. He could have taken one of three possible routes: along the coast, across the Jordan and up through Perea, or straight through Samaria. Orthodox Jews avoided Samaria because there was a long-standing, deep-seated hatred between them and the Samaritans.

The Samaritans were a mixed race, part Jew and part Gentile, that grew out of the Assyrian captivity of the ten northern tribes in 727 BC. Rejected by the Jews because they could not prove their genealogy, the Samaritans established their own temple and religious services on Mount Gerizim. This only fanned the fires of prejudice. So intense was their dislike of the Samaritans that some of the Pharisees prayed that no Samaritan would be raised in the resurrection! When His enemies wanted to call Jesus an insulting name, they called Him a Samaritan (John 8:48).

Because He was on a divinely appointed schedule, it was necessary that Jesus go through Samaria. Why? Because He would meet a woman there and lead her into saving faith, the kind of true faith that would affect an entire village. Our Lord was no respecter of persons. Earlier, He counseled a moral Jewish man (John 3), and now He would witness to an immoral Samaritan woman!

He arrived at Jacob's well around noon, the usual time for women to come for water. The disciples went to the nearby town for food while Jesus deliberately waited at the well. He was weary, hungry, and thirsty. John presents Jesus not only as the Son of God but also as true man. Our Lord entered into all the normal experiences of our lives and is able to identify with us in each of them.

As you read our Lord's interview with this woman, notice how her knowledge of Jesus increases until she acknowledges that He is the Christ. There were four stages in this experience.

(1) He is "a Jew" (vv. 7–10). In that day, it was not considered proper for any man, especially a rabbi, to speak in public to a strange woman (John 4:27). But our Lord set social customs aside because a soul's eternal salvation was at stake. It certainly surprised her when He asked for a drink of water. She surmised that He was a Jewish rabbi, and perhaps she tried to "read between the lines" to find another meaning to His request. What was He *really* seeking?

The information in John's parenthesis at the end of John 4:9 was for the benefit of his Gentile readers. Since the disciples had gone into the city to purchase food, it is obvious that the Jews did have *some* "dealings" with the Samaritans, so John was not trying to exaggerate. The phrase can be translated "ask no favors from the Samaritans" or "use no vessels in common with the Samaritans." Why would Jesus, a Jew, want to use her "polluted" vessel to get a drink of water?

Of course, our Lord's request was simply a way to open the conversation and share with her the truth about "living water." Whenever He witnessed to people, Jesus did not use a "sales talk" that He adapted to meet every situation. To Nicodemus, He spoke about new birth, but to this woman, He spoke about living water.

Jesus pointed out to her that she was ignorant of three important facts: who He was, what He had to offer, and how she could receive it. Here was eternal God speaking to her, offering her eternal life! The Samaritans were as blind as the Jews (John 1:26). But our Lord's words had aroused her interest, so she pursued the conversation.

(2) "Greater than Jacob" (vv. 11–15). Jesus was speaking about spiritual water, but she interpreted His words to mean literal water. Again, we see how easily people confuse the material and the spiritual. Furthermore, this woman was concerned about *how* He would obtain this water, instead of simply asking Him to give her a drink of it.

Of course Jesus *is* greater than Jacob—and greater than the well itself! To paraphrase His reply: "Whosoever *continues to drink* of this material water (or anything the world has to offer) will thirst again. But whosoever *takes one drink* of the water I give will never thirst again" (see John 4:13–14). How true it is that the things of this world never completely satisfy. In hell today, people are crying, "I thirst!"

We have noted before that *life* is one of John's key concepts. He uses the word at least thirty-six times. G. Campbell Morgan has pointed out that humankind needs air, water, and food in order to have life. (We might also add that humans needs light.) All of these are provided in Jesus Christ. He provides the "breath" (Spirit) of God (John 3:8; 20:22). He is the Bread of Life (John 6:48) and the Light of Life (John 1:4–5), and He gives us the water of life.

The woman's immediate response was to ask for this gift, but she did not know what she was saying. The seed of the Word fell on shallow soil, and the shoots that sprang up had no root (Matt. 13:20–21). She had made progress, but she still had a long way to go, so Jesus patiently dealt with her.

(3) **"A prophet" (vv. 16–24).** The only way to prepare the soil of the heart for the seed is to plow it up with conviction. That was why Jesus told her to go and get her husband: He forced her to admit her sin. There can be no conversion without conviction. There must first be conviction and repentance, and then there can be saving faith. Jesus had aroused her mind and stirred her emotions, but He also had to touch her conscience, and that meant dealing with her sin.

"I have no husband" was the shortest statement she made during the entire conversation! Why? Because now she was under conviction and her mouth was stopped (Rom. 3:19). But this was the best thing that could have happened to her!

However, instead of listening to Jesus, she tried to get Him on a "detour" by discussing the differences between the Jewish and the Samaritan religions. It is much more comfortable to discuss religion than to face one's sins! However, Jesus once again revealed her spiritual ignorance: She did not know who to worship, where to worship, or how to worship! He made it clear that all religions are not equally acceptable before God, that some worshippers act in ignorance and unbelief.

The only faith that God will accept is that which came through the

Jews. The Bible is of Jewish origin, and our Savior was a Jew. The first Christians were Jews. A religious worker in an airport told me that the world's deliverer came from Korea, but Jesus said, "Salvation is of the Jews." Only those who have the indwelling Holy Spirit and obey the truth can worship God acceptably.

It was a devastating statement to say that worship would no longer be limited to the Jewish temple. This ties in with John 2:19–21 and also Stephen's statement in Acts 7:48–50. John's gospel clearly reveals that there is a new sacrifice (John 1:29), a new temple (John 2:19–21; 4:20–24), a new birth (John 3:1–7), and a new water (John 4:11). Jews reading this gospel should realize that God has established in Jesus Christ a whole new economy. The old covenant law has been fulfilled and set aside.

(4) "The Christ" (vv. 25–30). In spite of her ignorance, there was one truth this woman did know: The Messiah was coming and would reveal the secrets of hearts. Where did she learn this truth? We do not know, but that seed had laid buried in her heart until that very hour, and now it was going to bear fruit. Our Lord's response to her statement was, literally, "I that speak to thee, I am!" He dared to utter the holy name of God!

At this point, the woman put her faith in Jesus Christ and was converted. Immediately she wanted to share her faith with others, so she went into the village and told the men she had met the Christ. When you consider how little spiritual truth this woman knew, her zeal and witness put us to shame. But God used her simple testimony, and many of the people came out to the well to meet Jesus. The rabbis said, "It is better that the words of the law be burned than be delivered to a woman!" But Jesus did not agree with that narrow prejudice.

Why did she leave her waterpot when she hurried into the city? For one thing, she had the living water within and was now satisfied. Also, she intended to come back, and perhaps in the interim, the disciples and Jesus could use the vessel to satisfy their thirst. Gone were the racial barriers and battles that had existed before! They were all one in faith and love!

This woman did not come to faith in Christ immediately. Jesus was patient with her, and in this, He sets a good example for us in our own personal work. Certainly she was the least likely prospect for salvation, yet God used her to win almost an entire village!

The Disciples (4:31–38)

When the disciples returned from obtaining food, they were shocked that Jesus was conversing with a woman, and especially a Samaritan, but they did not interrupt. They were learning that their Master knew what He was doing and did not need their counsel. But, after the woman left, they urged Jesus to share the meal with them, because they knew that He was hungry.

"I have meat to eat that ye know not of" was His reply, and, as usual, they did not understand it. They thought He was speaking of literal food, and they wondered where He got it. Then He explained that doing the Father's will—in this case, leading the woman to salvation—was true nourishment for His soul. The disciples were satisfied with bread, but He was satisfied with accomplishing the Father's work.

"Seek your life's nourishment in your life's work," said Phillips Brooks. The will of God ought to be a source of strength and satisfaction to the children of God, just as if they sat down to a sumptuous feast. If what we are doing tears us down instead of builds us up, then we may well question whether it is the will of God for us.

Our Lord did not look on the Father's will as a heavy burden or a distasteful task. He viewed His work as the very nourishment of His soul. Doing the Father's will fed Him and satisfied Him inwardly. "I delight to do thy will, O my God: yea, thy law is within my heart" (Ps. 40:8). The

Samaritan woman was now doing the Father's will and finding excitement and enrichment in it.

Jesus then changed the image from that of food to that of the harvest, which is the source of the food. He quoted the familiar Jewish proverb about waiting for the harvest and then pointed to the villagers even then coming out to the well to meet Him, thanks to the witness of the woman. The disciples went into the village to get food for themselves, but they did no evangelizing. The woman took their place!

The image of the harvest is a familiar one in the Bible and is often applied to the ministry of winning lost souls. Both the parable of the sower and the parable of the tares (Matt. 13:1–30) relate to this theme, and Paul used it in his letters (Rom. 1:13; 1 Cor. 3:6–9; Gal. 6:9). We plant the seed of God's Word in the hearts of people who hear it, and we seek to cultivate that seed by our love and prayers. In due time, that seed may bear fruit to the glory of God.

No doubt the disciples had said, as they approached the city of Sychar, "There can be no harvest here! These people despise us Jews and would have no use for our message." But just the opposite was true: The harvest was ready and only needed faithful workers to claim it. For some reason, when it comes to witnessing for Christ, it is always the wrong time and the wrong place! It takes faith to sow the seed, and we must do it even when the circumstances look discouraging. Read Ecclesiastes 11:4 and take it to heart!

There is no competition in the Lord's harvest. Each of us has an assigned task, and we are all a part of each other's labors (1 Cor. 3:6–9). One sows, one reaps, but each worker gets his honest reward for the work he has done.

John 4:38 indicates that others had labored in Samaria and had prepared the way for this harvest. We do not know who these faithful workers were, nor do we need to know, for God will reward them. Perhaps some of these people had heard John the Baptist preach, or perhaps some of John's followers had reached into this difficult field. Some archaeologists have located "Aenon near Salim" where John baptized (John 3:23) near the biblical Shechem, which is close to Sychar and Jacob's well. If this is the case, then John the Baptist prepared the soil and planted the seed, and Jesus and the disciples reaped the harvest. Of course, the woman herself planted some of the seed through her witness to the men.

The disciples were learning a valuable lesson that would encourage them in the years to come. They were not alone in the work of the Lord, and they must never look on any opportunity for witness as wasted time and energy. It takes faith to plow the soil and plant the seed, but God has promised a harvest (Ps. 126:5–6; Gal. 6:9). In a few years, Peter and John would participate in another harvest among the Samaritans (Acts 8:5–25). Those who sow may not see the harvest, but those who reap will see it and give thanks for the faithful labors of the sowers.

The Greek word translated "labor" in John 4:38 is translated "wearied" in John 4:6. Sowing, cultivating, and harvesting are difficult tasks, not only in the physical realm, but also in the spiritual realm. There is no place in the harvest for lazy people. The work is too difficult, and the laborers are too few.

The Samaritans (4:39–42)

Many of the Samaritans believed because of the testimony of the woman, and then many more believed when they heard Jesus personally. So excited were they about Him that they begged Him to stay with them, and He stayed for two days. During that short time, His word produced fruit in their lives.

It is important that new converts be grounded in the Word—the

Bible. These Samaritans began their spiritual walk by trusting in what the woman said, but they soon learned to trust the word taught by the Savior. Theirs was no "secondhand" salvation. They knew that they were saved because they had believed His message. "Now we know!" was their happy testimony.

You would have thought that these Samaritans would have been narrow in their faith, seeing Jesus as the Savior of the Jews and the Samaritans. But they declared that He was "the Savior of the world" (John 4:42). They had been converted only a few days, but they already had a missionary vision! In fact, their vision was wider than that of the apostles!

It is interesting to trace our Lord's movements that brought Him to Samaria. He was in Jerusalem (John 2:23) and then came into Judea (John 3:22). From Judea He went into Samaria (John 4:4), and the Samaritans declared Him to be "the Savior of the world." This is a perfect parallel to Acts 1:8—"And ye shall be witnesses unto me both in Jerusalem, and in all Judea, and in Samaria, and unto the uttermost part of the earth." Our Lord has set the example. If we follow, He will give us the harvest.

This unnamed Samaritan woman was a fruitful believer: She bore fruit ("many believed"), more fruit ("many more believed"), and today continues to bear "much fruit" to the glory of God (see John 15:1–5). Nobody knows how many lost sinners have come to the Savior because of the witness of this woman recorded in John 4.

THE NOBLEMAN (4:43–54)

Our Lord continued His journey to Galilee (John 4:3) and came again to Cana. Galilee was known as *"Galil ha goyim—Galilee of the Gentiles."* Apparently Jesus had detected in Judea (His own country) the increasing hostility of the religious leaders, though the real opposition would not yet appear for some months. Our Lord was really never identified with

Judea even though He had been born in Bethlehem. He was known as the prophet from Galilee (Matt. 21:11; John 7:52). Jesus knew that the public response to His ministry in Jerusalem had been insincere and shallow (John 2:23–25) and that it was not honoring to Him at all.

Why did Jesus return to Cana? Perhaps He wanted to cultivate the "seed" He had planted there when He attended the wedding feast. Nathanael came from Cana, so perhaps there was a personal reason for this visit. Jesus was met at Cana by a nobleman from Capernaum, some twenty miles away. The man had heard about His miracles and came all that distance to intercede for his son, who was dying. The first miracle at Cana came at the request of His mother (John 2:1–5), and this second miracle at Cana at the request of a father (John 4:47).

Was this man a Jew or a Gentile? We do not know. Nor do we know his exact position in the government. He may have been a member of Herod's court, but whatever his national or social standing, he was clearly at his wit's end and desperately needed the help of the Savior. He "kept beseeching him" to travel to Capernaum to heal his son.

John 4:48 was not a rebuke of this nobleman. Rather, it was our Lord's lament at the spiritual condition of the people in general, both in Judea and in Galilee. "Seeing is believing" has always been the "pragmatic" philosophy of the lost world, even the religious world. The nobleman believed that Jesus could heal his son, but he made two mistakes in his thinking: that Jesus had to go to Capernaum to save the lad and that if the boy died meanwhile, it was too late.

We must admire this man's faith. Jesus simply said, "Go thy way; thy son liveth" (John 4:50). And the man believed Jesus and started to return home! Both the Samaritan woman and this anonymous nobleman must have rejoiced the heart of Jesus as they believed the Word and acted on it.

The boy was healed the instant Jesus spoke those words, so the man's servants started out to find him so they could share the good news. (Again, it is the servants who know what is going on. See John 2:9; 15:15.) The boy had been healed at the seventh hour, which, in Roman time, would be seven o'clock in the evening. The father certainly would not have traveled at night, for that would have been dangerous; nor would the servants have taken that risk. The father's faith was so strong that he was willing to delay going home, even though his heart yearned to see his beloved son.

When the father and the servants met the next day, their report confirmed his faith. Note that the father thought the healing would be gradual ("began to improve"), but the servants reported a complete, instant recovery.

This man began with *crisis faith*. He was about to lose his son, and he had no other recourse but the Lord Jesus Christ. Many people came to Jesus with their crises, and He did not turn them away. The nobleman's crisis faith became *confident* faith: He believed the word and had peace in his heart. He was even able to delay his trip home, knowing that the boy was out of danger.

His confident faith became *confirmed* faith. Indeed, the boy had been completely healed! And the healing took place at the very time when Jesus spoke the word. It was this fact that made a believer out of the nobleman and his household. He believed that Jesus was the Christ, the Son of God, and he shared this faith with his family. He had *contagious* faith and shared his experience with others.

This is one of several miracles that Jesus performed "at a distance." He healed the centurion's servant from a distance (Matt. 8:5–13, and note that he too lived in Capernaum), and He healed the daughter of the Canaanite woman in the same manner (Matt. 15:21–28). These two were Gentiles and, spiritually speaking, were "at a distance" (Eph. 2:12–13). Perhaps this nobleman was also a Gentile. We do not know.

John 4:54 does not state that this healing was the second miracle that Jesus ever performed, for that would contradict John 2:23 and 3:2. This was the second miracle He performed *in Cana of Galilee* (see John 2:1, 11). He certainly gave those people special privileges.

But we must note that both miracles were "private" rather than public. Mary, the disciples, and the servants knew where the excellent wine had come from, but the guests did not. (Of course, it is possible that the servants told the story to others.) The nobleman's son was healed at Capernaum, not Cana, but news traveled rapidly in those days, and certainly the word got out.

Jesus' first miracle at the wedding revealed His power over *time*. The Father is always making water into wine, but He takes a season or two to finish the work. Jesus made the wine instantly. In this sense, our Lord's miracles were only *instantaneous* copies of what the Father is always doing. "My Father worketh hitherto, and I work" (John 5:17). The Father is constantly multiplying bread, season after season, but the Son multiplied it instantly.

In the second recorded miracle, Jesus showed His power over *space*. He was not limited simply because He was in Cana and the sick boy was in Capernaum. The fact that the father believed the word and did not know the results until the next day is evidence that he had confident faith. He trusted the word that Jesus spoke, and so should we.

QUESTIONS FOR PERSONAL REFLECTION OR GROUP DISCUSSION

1. What have you believed because of someone else's testimony?

2. Read verses 1–42. Jesus went through Samaria even though most Jewish people avoided it. What does this choice reveal about Him?

3. Why did Jesus ask the Samaritan woman for a drink?

4. How did she progress in her knowledge of who Jesus was?

5. Why do you suppose Jesus didn't tell her sooner that He was the Christ?

6. What do you learn about Jesus from the way He interacted with this sinful woman?

7. For her, faith led immediately to spreading the good news. Does faith have that effect on you? Why or why not?

8. Do you think it would be easier for you to tell unbelievers about Jesus if He were available in the flesh as He was in this story? Explain.

9. Read verses 43–54. How did the nobleman demonstrate his faith in Jesus?

10. What does this miracle teach us about Jesus?

11. How can you act on your faith as the Samaritan woman and the nobleman did?

Chapter Five

THE MAN WHO WAS EQUAL WITH GOD

(John 5)

Our Lord's first two miracles recorded by John were somewhat private in nature. The servants and the disciples knew that He transformed the water into wine, and the servants and the nobleman's family knew that He had healed the sick son. The miracle recorded in John 5 was not only public, but it was performed on the Sabbath day and incited the opposition of the religious leaders. We see here the beginning of "official persecution" against the Savior.

There are three exciting "acts" in this drama.

1. THE CURE (5:1–15)

When you visit St. Anne's Church in Jerusalem, they will show you the deep excavation that has revealed the ancient Pool of Bethesda. The Hebrew name *Bethesda* has been spelled various ways and given differing meanings. Some say it means "house of mercy" or "house of grace," but others say it means "place of the two outpourings." There is historical and archaeological evidence that two adjacent pools of water served this area in ancient times.

The pool is situated near the northeast corner of the Old City, close to the Sheep Gate (Neh. 3:1; 12:39). Perhaps John saw some spiritual significance to this location, for he had already told his readers that Jesus Christ is "the Lamb of God" (John 1:29).

We do not know which feast Jesus was observing when He went to Jerusalem, and it is not important that we know. His main purpose for going was not to maintain a religious tradition but to heal a man and use the miracle as the basis for a message to the people. The miracle illustrated what He said in John 5:24—the power of His word and the gift of life.

While it is true that some manuscripts omit the end of John 5:3 and all of verse 4, it is also true that the event (and the man's words in John 5:7) would make little sense if these words are eliminated. Why would anybody, especially a man sick for so many years, remain in one place if nothing special were occurring? You would think that after thirty-eight years of nothing happening to *anybody,* the man would go elsewhere and stop hoping! It seems wisest for us to accept the fact that something extraordinary kept all these people with disabilities at this pool, hoping for a cure.

John described these people as "impotent, blind, lame, paralyzed." What havoc sin has wrought in this world! But the healing of these infirmities was one of the prophesied ministries of the Messiah (Isa. 35:3–6). Had the religious leaders known their own Scriptures, they would have recognized their Redeemer, but they were spiritually blind.

No matter how you look at this miracle, it is an illustration of the grace of God. It was grace that brought Jesus to the Pool of Bethesda, for who would want to mingle with a crowd of helpless people?! Jesus did not heal all of them; He singled out one man and healed him. The fact that Jesus came to the man, spoke to him, healed him, and then met him later in the temple is proof of His wonderful grace and mercy.

John noted that the man had been ill for thirty-eight years. Perhaps he saw in this a picture of his own Jewish nation that had wandered in the wilderness for thirty-eight years (Deut. 2:14). Spiritually speaking, Israel was a nation of impotent people, waiting hopelessly for something to happen.

Jesus knew about the man (see John 2:23–24) and asked him if he wanted to be healed. You would think that the man would have responded with an enthusiastic, "Yes! I want to be healed!" But, instead, he began to give excuses! He had been in that sad condition for so long that his will was as paralyzed as his body. But if you compare John 5:6 with verse 40, you will see that Jesus had a spiritual lesson in mind as well. Indeed, this man did illustrate the tragic spiritual state of the nation.

The Lord healed him through the power of His spoken word. He commanded the man to do the very thing he was unable to do, but in His command was the power of fulfillment (see Mark 3:5; Heb. 4:12). The cure was immediate, and certainly some of the many people at the pool must have witnessed it. Jesus did not pause to heal anyone else; instead, He "conveyed himself away" (John 5:13) so as not to create a problem. (The Greek word means "to dodge.")

The miracle would have caused no problem except that it occurred on the Sabbath day. Our Lord certainly could have come a day earlier, or even waited a day, but He wanted to get the attention of the religious leaders. Later, He would deliberately heal a blind man on the Sabbath (John 9:1–14). The scribes had listed thirty-nine tasks that were prohibited on the Sabbath, and carrying a burden was one of them. Instead of rejoicing at the wonderful deliverance of the man, the religious leaders condemned him for carrying his bed and thereby breaking the law.

It is not easy to understand the relationship between this man and Jesus. There is no evidence that he believed on Christ and was converted, yet we cannot say that he was opposed to the Savior. In fact, he did not even know who it was that healed him until Jesus met him in the temple. No doubt the man went there to give thanks to God and to offer the appropriate sacrifices. It seems strange that the man did not actively seek a closer relationship with the One who healed him, but more than one person has gratefully accepted the gift and ignored the Giver.

Did the man "inform" on Jesus because of fear? We do not know. The Jewish leaders at least turned from him and aimed their accusations at Jesus Christ, and, unlike the healed blind man in John 9, this man was not excommunicated. The Lord's words (John 5:14) suggest that the man's physical plight had been the result of sin, but Jesus did not say that the man's sins had been forgiven as He did in dealing with the sick man lowered through the roof (see Mark 2:1–12). It is possible to experience an exciting miracle and still not be saved and go to heaven!

2. THE CONTROVERSY (5:16–18)

The Jewish leaders did not prosecute the man who was healed, even though he had broken the law, but they did begin to persecute the Lord Jesus. As the guardians of the faith, the members of the Jewish Sanhedrin (the religious ruling council) had the responsibility of investigating new preachers and teachers who appeared in the land, lest some false prophet come along and lead the people astray. They had looked into the ministry of John the Baptist (John 1:19ff.) and more recently had been scrutinizing the ministry of Jesus.

Jesus had healed a demoniac on the Sabbath (Luke 4:31–37), so the Sanhedrin was already suspicious. In the days following the miracle recorded in John 5, Jesus would defend His disciples for picking grain on the Sabbath (Matt. 12:1–8), and He would heal a man's withered hand on the Sabbath (Matt. 12:9–14). He deliberately challenged the legalistic traditions of the scribes and Pharisees. They had taken the Sabbath—God's gift to humanity—and had transformed it into a prison house of regulations and restrictions.

When they confronted Jesus with His unlawful conduct, He simply replied that He was doing only what His Father was doing! God's Sabbath rest had been broken by humanity's sin (see Gen. 3), and ever since the fall of humanity, God has been seeking lost sinners and saving them. But when Jesus said "my Father" instead of the usual "our Father," used by the Jews, He claimed to be equal with God.

The Jewish leaders instantly understood His claim, and they changed their accusation from that of Sabbath breaking to blasphemy, because Jesus claimed to be God. Liberal theologians who say that Jesus never claimed to be God have a difficult time with this passage.

Of course, the penalty for such blasphemy was death. It is here that the "official persecution" of Jesus began, culminating in His crucifixion. In the days that followed, our Lord often confronted His enemies with their evil desire to kill Him (John 7:19, 25; 8:37, 59). They hated Him without a cause (John 15:18–25). They ignored the good deeds that He performed for the helpless and hopeless and centered their attention on destroying Him.

Jesus made Himself equal with God because He is God. This is the theme of John's gospel. The Jewish leaders could not disprove His claims, so they tried to destroy Him and get Him out of the way. Both in His crucifixion and His resurrection, Jesus openly affirmed His deity and turned His enemies' weapons against them.

British writer George MacDonald pointed out that John 5:17 gives us a profound insight into our Lord's miracles. Jesus did *instantly* what the Father is always doing slowly. For example, in nature, as mentioned earlier, the Father is slowly turning water into wine, but Jesus did it instantly. Through the powers in nature, the Father is healing broken bodies, but Jesus healed them immediately. Nature is repeatedly multiplying bread, from sowing to harvest, but Jesus multiplied it instantly in His own hands.

3. The Claims (5:19–47)

In response to their accusations, Jesus made three significant claims that proved His sonship.

(1) He claimed to be equal with God (vv. 19–23). Instead of denying their accusation, He endorsed it! If today a man made this kind of a claim, we would conclude that he was joking or mentally disturbed. Jesus was certainly not insane, and there is every evidence that He was deadly serious when He spoke these words. Either He is what He claims to be, or He is a liar; and if He is a liar, how do you explain all the good He has done in the lives of needy people? Nobody wants to trust a liar; Jesus' disciples were willing to die for Him.

Jesus claimed to be one with His Father in *His works.* If healing a man on the Sabbath was a sin, then the Father was to blame! Jesus did nothing "of himself" but only that which the Father was doing. The Father and the Son worked together, doing the same deeds in the same way. "I and my Father are one" (John 10:30).

When our Lord came to earth as man, He submitted Himself to the Father in everything. "Lo, I come to do thy will, O God" (Heb. 10:9). He veiled His glory and laid aside the independent exercise of His divine attributes. In the wilderness, Satan tempted Him to use His divine powers for Himself, but He refused to act independently. He was totally dependent on the Father and the power of the Holy Spirit of God.

Not only did the Father show the Son His works and enable Him to do them, but the Father also shared His love (John 5:20). The first three gospels open with the Father calling Jesus "my beloved Son," and John echoed this statement in John 3:35. We usually think of the Father's love for the lost world, as in John 3:16, but we must also remember the Father's love for His dear Son.

Because the Father loves the Son, the Father shows Him His works.

The blind religious leaders could not see what Jesus was doing, because they did not know the Father or the Son. In fact, even greater works were in the Father's plan, works that would cause them to marvel. Perhaps He had in mind the healing of Lazarus, for in John 5:21, He mentioned the raising of the dead.

For Jesus to claim to have power to raise the dead was a blasphemous thing in the eyes of the Jewish leaders; they gave that power to God alone. They said that Jehovah held the three great keys: the key to open the heavens and give rain (Deut. 28:12); the key to open the womb and give conception (Gen. 30:22); and the key to open the grave and raise the dead (Ezek. 37:13). As far as the gospel records are concerned, Jesus had not yet raised anyone from the dead, so to make this claim was to invite even more opposition.

John 5:21 certainly can mean much more than the physical raising of people from the dead, for certainly Jesus was referring to His gift of spiritual life to the spiritually dead. He amplified this truth further as recorded in John 5:24–29.

So, Jesus claimed to be equal with the Father in His works, but He also claimed to be equal with the Father in *executing judgment* (John 5:22). To the orthodox Jew, Jehovah God was "the Judge of all the earth" (Gen. 18:25), and no one dared to apply that august title to himself. But Jesus did! By claiming to be the Judge, He claimed to be God. "Because he [God] hath appointed a day, in the which he will judge the world in righteousness by that man whom he hath ordained" (Acts 17:31).

Our Lord claimed equality in another area, namely, *equal honor with the Father* (John 5:23). The fact that He is the appointed Judge should cause people to honor Him. What a tremendous claim: If you do not honor the Son, you are not honoring the Father! The "religious" people who say that they worship God but deny the deity of Christ have neither the Father nor the Son! Apart from Jesus Christ, we cannot know the Father, worship the Father, or serve the Father.

(2) He claimed to have authority to raise the dead (vv. 24–29). For a second time, Jesus introduced His words with the solemn "verily, verily" (see John 5:19, 24–25). More than twenty times in John's gospel you will find Jesus using this solemn form of address. It is as though He was saying, "Pay attention to this! What I am about to say is important!"

In this fascinating paragraph, Jesus spoke about four different resurrections. He described the resurrection of lost sinners into eternal life (see John 5:24–25; Eph. 2:1–10). The lost sinner is as lifeless and helpless as a corpse. No matter how an undertaker may prepare a corpse, it is still dead, and no corpse is "deader" than any other corpse. If you are dead, you are dead! Lost sinners are helpless to save themselves, and they certainly cannot give themselves life.

How are dead sinners raised from the dead? By hearing God's Word and believing on God's Son. Jesus healed the paralyzed man at the pool by His Word (John 5:8). Each time He raised somebody from the dead, He spoke the Word (Luke 7:11–17; 8:49–56; John 11:41–44). His Word is "living and powerful" (Heb. 4:12 NKJV) and can raise sinners from spiritual death. "Everlasting life" means that they can never die spiritually again, nor can they ever come into judgment (Rom. 8:1). To hear His Word and believe means salvation; to reject His Word means condemnation (John 12:48).

The second resurrection mentioned is the resurrection of our Lord Himself (John 5:26). Our life is derived, but His life is original, "in himself." "In him was life" (John 1:4). The grave could not hold Him because He is "the Prince of life" (Acts 2:24; 3:15). Jesus laid down His life and then took it up again (John 10:17–18). Because He has life in Himself, He can share that life with all who will trust Him.

The third resurrection named is the future resurrection of life, when believers are raised from the dead (John 5:28–29a). This wonderful truth is explained in 1 Thessalonians 4:13–18 and 1 Corinthians 15. Keep in mind that resurrection is not reconstruction. It does not imply that God "puts the pieces back together again." The resurrection body is a new body, a glorified body, suited to the new heavenly environment. Death is not the end for the believer, nor will he or she live in heaven as a disembodied spirit. God saves the whole person, and this includes the body (Rom. 8:23; Phil. 3:20–21). This resurrection of life will take place when Jesus Christ returns in the air and calls His people to Himself.

The fourth resurrection He mentioned is the resurrection of condemnation (John 5:29b). This resurrection involves only the lost, and it will take place just before Jesus Christ ushers in the new heaven and the new earth (Rev. 20:11–15). What an awesome event that will be, when the dead "small and great" stand before Jesus Christ! The Father has committed all judgment to the Son (John 5:22) and has given Him the authority to execute judgment (John 5:27). Today Jesus Christ is the Savior, but one day He shall sit as the Judge.

The title "Son of man" used in John 5:27 refers to Daniel 7:13–14 and is a definite messianic title. It is used twelve times in John's gospel and over eighty times in all four gospels. The Jews would know this title from their reading of the book of Daniel, and they would know that by using it, Jesus was claiming to be the Messiah and the Judge.

Believers will be given resurrection bodies so that they might reign with Christ in glory. Unbelievers will be given resurrection bodies—but not glorified bodies—that they might be judged and then suffer punishment in those bodies. Bodies that were used for sin will suffer the consequences of that sin.

The fact that Jesus has the authority to raise the dead is proof that He is equal with the Father, and therefore He is God.

(3) He claimed that there are valid witnesses who support His claim to deity (vv. 30–47). The word *witness* is a key word in John's gospel; it is used forty-seven times. Jesus did bear witness to Himself, but He knew they would not accept it, so He called in three other witnesses.

The first was John the Baptist (John 5:30–35), whom the religious leaders had interrogated carefully (John 1:15ff.). In fact, at the very end of His ministry, our Lord pointed the rulers back to the witness of John the Baptist (Matt. 21:23–27). John knew who Jesus was and faithfully declared what he knew to the people of Israel. John told the people that Jesus was the Lord (John 1:23), the Lamb of God (John 1:29, 36), and the Son of God (John 1:34).

John was a "burning and a shining lamp" (Jesus is the Light, John 8:12), and the Jewish people were excited about his ministry. However, their enthusiasm cooled, and nobody lifted a finger to try to deliver John when he was arrested by Herod. The leaders looked on John as a "local celebrity" (Matt. 11:7–8), but they did not want to receive his message of repentance. The publicans and sinners accepted John's message and were converted, but the religious leaders refused to submit (Matt. 21:28–32).

Whenever God raises up a spiritual leader who commands attention, there is always the danger of attracting people who want to bask in his popularity but not submit to his authority. A "mixed multitude" followed Moses and Israel out of Egypt, people who were impressed with the miracles but not yielded to the Lord. The prophets and apostles, as well as the great leaders in church history, all had to put up with shallow people who followed the crowd but refused to obey the truth. We have them in churches today.

Our Lord's second witness was the witness of His miracles (John 5:36). You will remember that John selected seven of these "signs" to include in his gospel as proof that Jesus is the Son of God (John 20:30–31). Jesus made it clear that His works were the works of the Father (John 5:17–20; 14:10). Even Nicodemus had to admit that our Lord's miracles identified Him as sent from God (John 3:2).

But the Bible also records miracles performed by ordinary men, such as Moses, Elijah, and Paul. Do these miracles prove that they are also sent of God? Yes, they do (see Heb. 2:3–4), but none of these men ever claimed to be the very Son of God. No servant of God able to perform God's mighty works would ever claim to be God Himself. The fact that Jesus made this claim, backed up by His mighty works and perfect life, is evidence that His claim is true.

Jesus indicated that the Father gave Him a specific ministry to finish while He was here on earth. "I have finished the work which thou gavest me to do" (John 17:4). He was not only on a divine timetable, but He followed a divine agenda. He had specific works to accomplish in the Father's will.

Since the Old Testament law required the testimony of two or three witnesses (Num. 35:30; Deut. 17:6), the Lord met that requirement by giving three trustworthy witnesses.

The third and final witness our Lord summoned was *the Word of the Father* (John 5:37–47). The Jewish people highly revered the written Word of God, particularly the law that was given through Moses. Moses heard God's voice and saw God's glory, but we have that same voice and glory in the inspired Word of God (see 2 Peter 1:12–21). The Old Testament Scriptures bear witness to Jesus Christ, yet the people who received and preserved that Word were blind to their own Messiah. Why?

For one thing, they did not permit that Word to generate faith in their hearts (John 5:38). John 5:39 is probably a statement of fact and not a command and could be rendered: "Ye search the scriptures, for in them ye think ye have eternal life." The Jewish scribes sought to know the Word of God, but they did not know the God of the Word! They counted the very letters of the text, but they missed the spiritual truths that the text contained.

Because of my radio ministry, I often receive letters from people who disagree with my interpretations or applications of Scripture, and sometimes these letters are quite angry. (I will not quote here the language I have seen in letters from professed Christians!) It is unfortunate when our "study" of the Bible makes us arrogant and militant instead of humble and anxious to serve others, even those who disagree with us. The mark of true Bible study is not knowledge that puffs up, but love that builds up (1 Cor. 8:1).

So, there was something wrong with the *minds* of these Jewish leaders: They did not see Christ in their own Scriptures (see 2 Cor. 3:14–18; 4:3–6). But there was also something wrong with their *wills:* They would not trust in the Savior. Because they did not have the Word in their hearts, they did not want Christ in their hearts. They were religious and self-righteous, but they were not saved.

These leaders had a third problem, and this was the lack of love in their *hearts.* "Ye have not the love of God in you" (John 5:42). This means the experience of God's love for them as well as their expression of love for God. They claimed to love God, but their attitude toward Jesus Christ proved that their love was counterfeit.

Their attitude toward God's Word hindered their faith, but so also did their attitude toward themselves and one another. The Pharisees enjoyed being honored by men (see Matt. 23:1–12), and they did not seek for the honor that comes from God alone. They did not honor the Son (John 5:23) because He did not honor them! Because they rejected the true Son of God who came in the Father's name, they would one day accept a false messiah, the Antichrist, who would come in his own name (John 5:43; and see 2 Thess. 2; Rev. 13). If we reject that which is true, we will ultimately receive that which is false.

Our Lord closed this penetrating sermon by warning the Jewish leaders that Moses, whom they honored, would be their judge, not their savior. The very Scriptures that they used to defend their religion would one day bear witness against them. The Jews *knew* what Moses wrote, but they did not really *believe* what he wrote. It is one thing to have the Word in our hands or our heads, but quite another thing to have it in our hearts. Jesus is the Word made flesh (John 1:14), and the written Word bears witness to the incarnate Word. "And beginning at Moses and all the prophets, he expounded unto them in all the scriptures the things concerning himself" (Luke 24:27).

The witness of John the Baptist, the witness of the divine miracles, and the witness of the Word of God all unite to declare that Jesus Christ is indeed one with the Father and the very Son of God.

Our Lord was not intimidated by the accusations of the religious leaders. If you check a harmony of the Gospels, you will see that after the events recorded in John 5, Jesus deliberately violated the Sabbath again! He permitted His disciples to pick grain on the Sabbath, and He healed a man with a withered hand (Matt. 12:1–14). These events probably took place in Galilee, but the news would certainly reach the leaders in Jerusalem and Judea.

The healing of the man on the Sabbath would come up again (John 7:21–23). The leaders would persist in protecting tradition instead of understanding truth (see Mark 7:1–13). But before we judge them, perhaps we ought to examine our own lives and churches. Are we permitting religious tradition to blind us to the truth of God's Word? Are we so involved in "Bible study" that we fail to see Jesus Christ in the Word? Does our knowledge of the Bible give us a "big head" or a "burning heart"?

QUESTIONS FOR PERSONAL REFLECTION
OR GROUP DISCUSSION

1. What unwritten rules does your church or denomination have (e.g., dancing is wrong)?

2. Read verses 1–15. The Pharisees in Jesus' day had a lot of rules too, including what not to do on the Sabbath. Why do you suppose Jesus deliberately flouted those rules and healed on the Sabbath?

3. Does it ever bother you when Jesus doesn't do things the way you think He should? If so, give an example.

4. How can you keep from letting your prejudices (such as about how things ought to be done) hinder you from seeing and responding to what God is doing in the world?

5. Read verses 16–47. In what ways did Jesus claim to be equal to God?

6. If someone came to your church and claimed to be equal to God, what evidence would you need to be convinced?

7. What witnesses did Jesus present to back up His claims?

8. Would those witnesses convince you if someone produced them at your church in support of such lofty claims? Why or why not?

9. How strong is the love of God in your heart? What makes you say that?

10. How can you strengthen that love?

Chapter Six

JESUS LOSES HIS CROWD

(John 6)

Since John's gospel is selective (John 20:30–31), he does not record events in the life of Jesus that do not help him fulfill his purpose. Between the healing of the paralytic (John 5) and the feeding of the five thousand, you have many events taking place, some of which are mentioned in Luke 6:1—9:10 and Mark 3:1—6:30. During this period our Lord preached the Sermon on the Mount (Matt. 5—7) and gave the parables of the kingdom (Matt. 13).

The feeding of the five thousand was a miracle of such magnitude that it is recorded in all four gospels. A great multitude had been following Jesus for several days, listening to His teaching and beholding His miracles. Jesus had tried to "get away" to rest, but the needs of the crowd pressed on Him (Mark 6:31–34). Because of His compassion, He ministered to the multitude in three different ways.

1. JESUS FEEDS THE MULTITUDE (6:1–14)

The problem, of course, was how to meet the needs of such a vast crowd of people. Four solutions were proposed.

First, the disciples suggested that Jesus send the people away (Mark

6:35–36). Get rid of the problem (see Matt. 15:23). But Jesus knew that the hungry people would faint on the way if somebody did not feed them. It was evening (Matt. 14:15), and that was no time for travel.

The second solution came from Philip in response to our Lord's "test question" (John 6:5): Raise enough money to buy food for the people. Philip "counted the cost" and decided they would need the equivalent of two hundred days' wages! And even that would not provide bread enough to satisfy the hunger of all the men, women, and children (Matt. 14:21). Too often, we think that money is the answer to every need. Of course, Jesus was simply testing the strength of Philip's faith.

The third solution came from Andrew, but he was not quite sure how the problem would be solved. He found a little boy who had a small lunch: two little fish and five barley cakes. Once again, Andrew is busy bringing somebody to Jesus (see John 1:40–42; 12:20–22). We do not know how Andrew met this lad, but we are glad he did! Though Andrew does not have a prominent place in the Gospels, he was apparently a "people person" who helped solve problems.

The fourth solution came from our Lord, and it was the true solution. He took the little boy's lunch, blessed it, broke it, handed it out to His disciples, and they fed the whole crowd! The miracle took place in the hands of the Savior, not in the hands of the disciples. He multiplied the food; they only had the joyful privilege of passing it out. Not only were the people fed and satisfied, but the disciples salvaged twelve baskets of fragments for future use. The Lord wasted nothing.

The practical lesson is clear: Whenever there is a need, give all that you have to Jesus, and let Him do the rest. Begin with what you have, but be sure you give it all to Him. That little lad is to be commended for sharing his lunch with Christ, and his mother is to be commended for giving him something to give to Jesus. The gift of that little snack meant as much to Jesus as the pouring out of the expensive ointment (John 12:1ff.).

But did Jesus really perform a miracle? Perhaps the generosity of the boy only embarrassed the other people so that they brought out their hidden lunches and shared them all around. Nonsense! Jesus knows people's hearts (John 2:24; 6:61, 64, 70), and He declared that the people were hungry. Surely He would have known of the existence of hidden food! Furthermore, the people themselves declared that this was a miracle and even wanted to crown Him King (John 6:14–16)! Had this event been only the result of mass psychology, the crowd would not have responded that way. John would never have selected this as one of the "signs" if it were not an authentic miracle.

It is significant that twice John mentioned the fact that Jesus gave thanks (John 6:11, 23). Matthew, Mark, and Luke all state that Jesus looked up to heaven when He gave thanks. By that act, He reminded the hungry people that God is the source of all good and needful gifts. This is a good lesson for us: Instead of complaining about what we do not have, we should give thanks to God for what we do have, and He will make it go further.

2. Jesus Leaves the Multitude (6:15–21)

Jesus compelled the disciples to get into the boat (Matt. 14:22; Mark 6:45) because He knew they were in danger. The crowd was now aroused, and there was a movement to make Him King. Of course, some of the disciples would have rejoiced at the opportunity to become famous and powerful! Judas would have become treasurer of the kingdom, and perhaps Peter would have been named prime minister! But this was not in the plan of God, and Jesus broke up the meeting immediately. Certainly the Roman government would have stepped in had a movement begun.

Did Jesus know that a storm was coming? Of course. Then why did He deliberately send His friends into danger? Quite the opposite is true: He was rescuing them from greater danger, the danger of being swept along by a fanatical crowd. But there was another reason for that storm: The Lord has to balance our lives; otherwise, we will become proud and then fall. The disciples had experienced great joy in being part of a thrilling miracle. Now they had to face a storm and learn to trust the Lord more. The feeding of the five thousand was the lesson, but the storm was the examination after the lesson.

Sometimes we are caught in a storm because we have disobeyed the Lord. Jonah is a good example. But sometimes the storm comes because we have *obeyed* the Lord. When that happens, we can be sure that our Savior will pray for us, come to us, and deliver us. In writing the account of this event years later, perhaps John saw in it a picture of Christ and His church. Christ is in heaven interceding for us, but we are in the midst of the storms of life, trying to reach the shore. One day, He will come for us and we shall reach the port safely, the storms all past.

Actually, there were several miracles involved in this event. Jesus walked on the water, and so did Peter (Matt. 14:28–32). Jesus stilled the storm, and instantly the boat was on the other shore. Of course, all of this happened at night so that only Jesus and His disciples knew what had occurred. Jesus had led His people into the green pastures (John 6:10), and now He brought them into the still waters (Ps. 23:2). What a wonderful Shepherd He is!

As you read the gospel records, note that our Lord was never impressed by the great crowds. He knew that their motives were not pure and that most of them followed Him in order to watch His miracles of healing. "Bread and circuses" was Rome's formula for keeping the people happy, and people today are satisfied with that kind of diet. Give them food and entertainment, and they are happy. Rome set aside ninety-three days each year for public games at government expense. It was cheaper to entertain the crowds than to fight them or jail them.

We must never be deceived by the "popularity" of Jesus Christ among certain kinds of people today. Very few want Him as Savior and Lord. Many want Him only as Healer or Provider or the One who rescues them from problems they have made for themselves. "And ye will not come to me, that ye might have life" (John 5:40).

3. Jesus Teaches the Multitude (6:22–71)

The purpose of the sign was that He might preach the sermon. Again, it was a ministry of "grace and truth" (John 1:17). In grace, our Lord fed the hungry people, but in truth, He gave them the Word of God. They wanted the food, but they did not want the truth; and, in the end, most of them abandoned Jesus and refused to walk with Him. He lost His crowd with one sermon!

The next day began with a mystery: How did Jesus get to Capernaum? The crowd saw the disciples embark to go across the Sea of Galilee to Capernaum, and then the men were lost in the storm. The crowd also saw Jesus leave the place and go by Himself to a mountain. But the next morning, here were Jesus and His disciples *together* in Capernaum! Certainly He had not walked around the lake, and there was no evidence that He had taken another boat. Other boats had arrived, no doubt driven in by the storm, but Jesus had not been in any of them.

No doubt some of the people who had been fed simply went away to their homes, while others stayed to see what Jesus would do next. Our Lord's sermon probably began outdoors, and then the discussion moved into the synagogue (John 6:59). It would be impossible for a huge crowd to participate in the synagogue service, though the overflow could remain outside and hear what was being said.

This sermon on "the bread of life" is actually a dialogue between Christ and the people, especially the religious leaders ("the Jews"). We see four responses of the crowd to the Lord Jesus in John 6: seeking (vv. 22–40), murmuring (vv. 41–51), striving (vv. 52–59), and departing (vv. 60–71).

(1) Seeking (vv. 22–40). The disciples may have been impressed that so many people stayed through a storm in order to seek their Master, but Jesus was not impressed. He knows the human heart. He knew that the people originally followed Him because of His miracles (John 6:2), but now their motive was to get fed! Even if they were attracted only by the miracles, at least there was still a possibility they might be saved. After all, that is where Nicodemus started (John 3:1–2). But now their interest had degenerated to the level of food.

Jesus pointed out that there are two kinds of food: food for the body, which is necessary but not the most important, and food for the inner man, the spirit, which is essential. What the people needed was not food but *life,* and life is a gift. Food only *sustains* life, but Jesus *gives* eternal life. The words of Isaiah come to mind: "Why do you spend money for what is not bread, and your wages for what does not satisfy?" (Isa. 55:2 NASB).

The people picked up the word *labor* and misinterpreted it to mean they had to *work* for salvation. They completely missed the word *give.* Steeped in legalistic religion, they thought they had to "do something" to merit eternal life. Jesus made it clear that only one "work" was necessary—to believe in the Savior. When people believe in Christ, they are not performing a good work that earns them salvation. There is certainly no credit in believing, for it is what God does *in response to our faith* that is important (see Eph. 2:8–10).

The crowd began by seeking Christ, but then started to seek a sign from Him. "For the Jews require a sign" (1 Cor. 1:22). The rabbis taught that, when Messiah came, He would duplicate the miracle of the manna (see Ex. 16). If Jesus was truly sent by God (see John 6:29, 38, 57), then let

Him prove it by causing manna to fall from heaven. They wanted to "see and believe." But faith that is based on signs alone, and not on the truth of the Word, can lead a person astray, for even Satan is able to perform "lying wonders" (2 Thess. 2:8–10). Note also John 2:18–25; 4:48.

The quotation in John 6:31 is from Psalm 78:24, a psalm that records the unbelief and rebellion of the nation of Israel.

In His reply, our Lord sought to deepen the people's understanding of the truth. It was *God,* not Moses, who gave the manna, so they must take their eyes off Moses and focus them on God. Also, God *gave* the manna in the past, but the Father is *now giving* the true bread in the person of Jesus Christ. The past event is finished, but the present spiritual experience goes on!

Then Jesus clearly identified what the bread is: He is the true Living Bread that came down from heaven. But He came, not only for Israel but also for the whole world. And He came, not just to *sustain* life, but to *give* life! Seven times in this sermon, our Lord referred to His "coming down from heaven" (John 6:33, 38, 41–42, 50–51, 58), a statement that declared Him to be God. The Old Testament manna was but a type of the "true bread," the Lord Jesus Christ.

This dialogue began with the crowd seeking Christ and then seeking a sign, but listeners soon began to seek the "true bread" that Jesus talked about. However, like the woman of Samaria, they were not ready for salvation (see John 4:15). She wanted the living water so she would not have to keep going to the well. The crowd wanted the bread so they would not have to toil to maintain life. People today still want Jesus Christ only for the benefits He is able to give.

In His reply to their impetuous request, Jesus used two key words that often appear in this sermon: *come* and *believe.* To come to Jesus means to believe in Him, and to believe in Him means to come to Him. Believing is not merely an intellectual thing, giving mental assent to some doctrine. It means to come to Christ and yield yourself to Him. At the close of His sermon, Jesus illustrated *coming* and *believing* by speaking about *eating* and *drinking*. To come to Christ and believe in Him means to receive Him within, just as you receive food and drink.

John 6:35 contains the first of seven great "I am" statements recorded by John, statements that are found nowhere else in the Gospels. (For the other six, see John 8:12; 10:7–9, 11–14; 11:25–26; 14:6; 15:1, 5.) God revealed Himself to Moses by the name I AM (Jehovah) (Ex. 3:14). God is the self-existent One who "is, and … was, and … is to come" (Rev. 1:8). When Jesus used the name "I am," He was definitely claiming to be God.

John 6:37–40 contains Jesus' explanation of the process of personal salvation. These are among the most profound words He ever spoke, and we cannot hope to plumb their depths completely. He explained that salvation involves both divine sovereignty and human responsibility. The Father *gives* men and women to the Son (John 6:37, 39; 17:2, 6, 9, 11–12, 24), but these men and women must *come* to Him, that is, *believe* in Him. He assured them that nobody who came to Him would ever be lost but would be raised at the last day. Even death cannot rob us of salvation! (In regard to the "last day," see John 6:40, 44, 54. Jesus was referring to His return and the final events that climax God's program for humanity.)

From our human and limited perspective, we cannot see how divine sovereignty and human responsibility can work together, but from God's perspective, there is no conflict. When a church member asked Charles Spurgeon how he reconciled these two, he replied, "I never try to reconcile friends." It is the Father's will that sinners be saved (1 Tim. 2:4; 2 Peter 3:9) and that those who trust Christ be secure in their salvation. Believers receive eternal life, and Jesus can never lose them.

(2) Murmuring (vv. 41–51). Our Lord's statement "For I came down from heaven" (John 6:38) disturbed the religious leaders, for they knew it was a claim of deity. They thought they knew Jesus, who He was and where He came from (see Matt. 13:53–58; John 7:40–43). Jesus, of course, was the *legal* son of Joseph but not his natural son, for He was born of a virgin (Luke 1:34–38). The leaders identified Jesus with Nazareth in Galilee, not Bethlehem in Judea, and they thought that Joseph was His natural father. Had they investigated the matter, they would have learned who Jesus really is.

Even in the days of Moses, the Jews were known for their murmuring (Ex. 15:24; 17:3; Num. 14:2). Perhaps the leaders and some of the crowd had now moved into the synagogue to continue the discussion. The main issue was, "Where did He come from?" Five times Jesus used the phrase "came down from heaven," but they would not accept it.

Jesus further explained how the sinner can come to God: It is through the truth of the Word (John 6:44–45). The Father draws the sinner by His Word. Jesus quoted Isaiah 54:13 (or perhaps Jer. 31:33–34) to prove His point: "And [they] shall be taught of the LORD." It is through the teaching of the Word that God draws people to the Savior. (Note John 5:24 and its emphasis on hearing the Word.) The sinner hears, learns, and comes as the Father draws him or her. A mystery? Yes! A blessed reality? Yes!

This was basically the same message He gave after He had healed the paralytic (see John 5:37–40). The crowd wanted to *see* something, but their real need was to *learn* something. It is by the Word that we "see" God and receive the faith to come to Christ and trust Him (Rom. 10:17).

When Jesus called Himself the Living Bread, He was not claiming to be exactly like the manna. *He was claiming to be even greater!* The manna only *sustained life* for the Jews, but Jesus *gives life* to the whole world. The Jews ate the daily manna and eventually died, but when you receive Jesus Christ within, you live forever. When God gave the manna, He gave only a gift, but when Jesus came, He gave Himself. There was no cost to God in sending the manna each day, but He gave His Son at great cost. The Jews had to eat the manna every day, but the sinner who trusts Christ *once* is given eternal life.

It is not difficult to see in the manna a picture of our Lord Jesus Christ. The manna was a mysterious thing to the Jews; in fact, the word *manna* means "What is it?" (see Ex. 16:15). Jesus was a mystery to those who saw Him. The manna came at night from heaven, and Jesus came to this earth when sinners were in moral and spiritual darkness. The manna was small (His humility), round (His eternality), and white (His purity). It was sweet to the taste (Ps. 34:8), and it met the needs of the people adequately.

The manna was given to a rebellious people; it was the gracious gift of God. All they had to do was stoop and pick it up. If they failed to pick it up, *they walked on it.* The Lord is not far from any sinner. All the sinner has to do is humble himself or herself and take the gift that God offers.

Jesus closed this part of His message by referring to His *flesh*, a word that will be used six more times before the dialogue is concluded. John 6:51 is a declaration that the Son of God will give Himself as a sacrifice "for the life of the world." The substitutionary death of Jesus Christ is a key doctrine in John's gospel. Jesus would die for the world (John 3:16; 6:51), for His sheep (John 10:11, 15), for the nation (John 11:50–52), and for His friends (John 15:12–13). Paul made it personal, and so should we: "who loved me, and gave himself for me" (Gal. 2:20). We must not limit the work of Christ on the cross. He is the sacrifice not only for our sins, but also for the sins of the whole world (1 John 2:2).

(3) Striving (vv. 52–59). The word *striving* means "to fight and quarrel." Being orthodox Jews, the listeners knew the divine prohibition against eating human flesh or any kind of blood (Gen. 9:3–4; Lev. 17:10–16; 19:26). Here we have another example in John's gospel of the people misunderstanding a spiritual truth by treating it literally (see John 2:19–21; 3:4; 4:11). All Jesus said was, "Just as you take food and drink within your body and it becomes a part of you, so you must receive Me within your innermost being so that I can give you life."

Some interpreters tell us that Jesus was speaking about the Lord's Supper and that we eat His flesh and drink His blood when we partake of the elements at the table, the bread and the cup. I do not believe that Jesus had Communion (or Eucharist) in mind when He spoke these words.

For one thing, why would He discuss the Lord's Supper with a group of disagreeable unbelievers? He had not even shared that truth with His own disciples! Why would He cast this precious pearl before the swine?

Second, He made it clear that He was not speaking in literal terms (John 6:63). He was using a human analogy to convey a spiritual truth, just as He did with Nicodemus and the Samaritan woman.

Third, Jesus made it plain that this eating and drinking were *absolutely essential* for eternal life. He made no exceptions. If, then, He was speaking about a church ordinance (or sacrament), then everybody who has never shared in that experience is spiritually dead and is going to hell. This would include all the Old Testament saints, the thief on the cross, and a host of people who have trusted Christ in emergency situations (hospitals, accidents, foxholes, etc.). I personally cannot believe that our gracious God has excluded from salvation all who cannot participate in a church ceremony.

Another factor is the tense of the Greek verbs in John 6:50–51 and 53. It is the aorist tense, which signifies a once-for-all action. The Communion service is a repeated thing; in fact, it is likely that the early church observed the Lord's Supper daily (Acts 2:46).

It is significant that the word *flesh* is never used in any of the reports of the Lord's Supper, either in the Gospels or in 1 Corinthians 11:23–34. The word used is *body*.

If a person holds that our Lord was speaking about the Communion service, then he or she must believe that somehow the two elements, the bread and the fruit of the vine, turn into the very body and blood of Christ, for He said, "So he that eateth *me,* even he shall live by *me"* (John 6:57). How does this "miracle" take place? What is the secret of accomplishing it? Why is it not apparent?

Our Lord's messages recorded in the gospel of John are filled with symbolism and imagery. To take them literally is to make the same mistake the people made who first heard them.

(4) Departing (vv. 60–71). Our Lord's teaching was not hard to understand but hard to accept once you understood it. The Jewish religious leaders both misunderstood His words and rejected them. They were "offended" by what He taught. (The Greek word is "scandaled.") They stumbled over the fact that He claimed to come down from heaven. They also stumbled over the idea that they had to eat His flesh and drink His blood in order to be saved. But if they stumbled over these two matters, what would they do if they saw Him ascend back into heaven (John 6:62)?

Jesus explained that His language was figurative and spiritual, not literal. There is no salvation in "flesh." In fact, the New Testament has nothing good to say about "the flesh." There is nothing good in it (Rom. 7:18), and we must not have confidence in it (Phil. 3:3).

How, then, do we "eat His flesh and drink His blood"? *Through the Word.* "The words that I speak unto you, they are spirit, and they are life" (John 6:63). "And the Word was made flesh" (John 1:14). Our Lord said the same thing: "He that heareth my word, and believeth on him that sent me, hath everlasting life" (John 5:24). The scribes who knew Jeremiah 31:31–34 would have understood the concept of receiving God's Word into one's inner being.

The result of this message was the loss of most of our Lord's disciples. They went back to the old life, the old religion, and the old hopeless situation. Jesus Christ is "the way" (John 14:6), but they would not walk with Him. This was no surprise to the Lord, because He knows the hearts of all people.

When Jesus asked His twelve apostles if they planned to desert Him too, it was Peter who spoke up and declared their faith. Where else could they go? "Thou hast the words of eternal life." Peter got the message! He knew that Jesus was speaking about *the Word* and not about literal flesh and blood.

Peter was one of several people who declared their belief that Jesus is the Son of God (see John 1:34, 49; 3:18; 5:25; 9:35; 10:36; 11:4, 27; 19:7; 20:31). The only mistake he made was to bear witness for the entire group. Peter was sure that *all* of the apostles were believers, which shows how convincing Judas was. Even Peter did not know that Judas was an unbeliever!

The preaching of the Word of God always leads to a sifting of the hearts of the listeners. God draws sinners to the Savior through the power of truth, His Word. Those who reject the Word will reject the Savior. Those who receive the Word will receive the Savior and experience the new birth, eternal life.

Do you feel your need because there is a spiritual hunger within? Are you willing to admit that need and come to the Savior? If you will, He will save you and satisfy you *forever!*

QUESTIONS FOR PERSONAL REFLECTION
OR GROUP DISCUSSION

1. What's your first reaction when you face an impossible situation?

2. Read verses 1–14. How easy is it for you to give all you have to Jesus when there's a problem to solve? Why is that?

3. Does the story of the miraculous feeding motivate you to do this? Explain.

4. Read verses 15–21. Why did Jesus deliberately send His disciples into the danger of the storm?

5. When, if ever, has pride at success been a problem for you? How did God address that with you?

6. Read verses 22–71. Was wanting physical food a good reason to seek Jesus? Explain.

7. What did Jesus mean when He said, "I am the bread of life"?

8. Why was "eat my flesh and drink my blood" (v. 54 NIV) a hard teaching for these potential disciples to accept?

9. How easy is it for you to live by this teaching? Why?

10. How does Jesus want you to respond the next time you face an impossible situation or a truth that is hard to accept?

Chapter Seven

FEAST FIGHT

(John 7)

The Feast of Tabernacles looked back to Israel's journey through the wilderness and looked forward to the promised kingdom of Messiah. The Jews lived in booths made of branches to remind them of God's providential care of the nation for nearly forty years (Lev. 23:33–44).

Following the Feast of Trumpets and the solemn Day of Atonement, Tabernacles was a festive time for the people. The temple area was illumined by large candlesticks that reminded the people of the guiding pillar of fire, and each day the priests would carry water from the Pool of Siloam and pour it out from a golden vessel, reminding the Jews of the miraculous provision of water from the rock.

The feast may have been a jubilant time for the people, but it was a difficult time for Jesus, for it marked the beginning of open and militant opposition to Him and His ministry. Ever since He had healed the paralytic on the Sabbath day, Jesus had been targeted by the Jewish leaders who wanted to kill Him (John 7:1, 19–20, 25, 30, 32, 44; and note 8:37, 40). He remained in Galilee, where He would be safer, but He could not remain in Galilee and also observe the feast.

John 7 has three time divisions: before the feast (vv. 1–10), in the midst of the feast (vv. 11–36), and on the last day of the feast (vv. 37–52). The responses during each of those periods can be characterized by three words: disbelief, debate, and division.

1. Before the Feast: Disbelief (7:1–10)

Mary bore other children, with Joseph as their natural father (Matt. 13:55–56; Mark 6:1–6), so Jesus would have been their half brother. It seems incredible that His brothers could have lived with Him all those years and not realized the uniqueness of His person. Certainly they knew about His miracles (see John 7:3–4) since everybody else did. Having been in the closest contact with Him, they had the best opportunity to watch Him and test Him, yet they were still unbelievers.

Here were men going up to a religious feast yet rejecting their own Messiah! How easy it is to follow tradition and miss eternal truth. The publicans and sinners were rejoicing at His message, but His own half brothers were making fun of Him.

These men certainly had the world's point of view: If you want to get a following, use your opportunities to do something spectacular. Jerusalem would be crowded with pilgrims, and this would give Jesus the ideal "platform" to present Himself and win disciples. No doubt the brothers knew that the multitude of disciples had deserted Jesus (John 6:66). This was His opportunity to recoup His losses. Satan had offered a similar suggestion three years before (Matt. 4:1ff.).

Jesus had already turned down the crowd's offer to make Him King (John 6:15), and He was not about to yield to them in any way. Celebrities might ride to success on the applause of the crowd, but God's servants know better. By doing miracles during the feast, at the "official city," Jesus could muster a crowd, reveal Himself as Messiah, and overcome the enemy. The suggestion, of course, came from hearts and minds blinded by unbelief. This unbelief had been prophesied in Psalm 69:8—"I am become a stranger unto my brethren, and an alien unto my mother's children." (Since Jesus was not Joseph's natural son, He could not say, "My father's children.")

It was not the right time for Jesus to show Himself to the world (John 14:22ff.). One day He shall return, and "every eye shall see him" (Rev. 1:7). We have noticed that our Lord lived on a "divine timetable" that was marked out by the Father (John 2:4; 7:6, 8, 30; 8:20; 12:23; 13:1; 17:1).

Jesus was exercising caution because He knew that the Jewish leaders wanted to kill Him. Though they were "religious" leaders, they were a part of "the world" that hated Jesus because He exposed their evil works. By His character and His ministry, He revealed the shallowness and emptiness of their futile religious system; He called the people back to the reality of life in God. History reveals that the "religious system" often persecutes the very prophets of God who are sent to save it!

Some manuscripts do not have the word *yet* in John 7:8, but its absence does not alter the thrust of the statement. Jesus was certainly not lying or being evasive; rather, He was exercising sensible caution. Suppose He told His brothers His plans and they told somebody else? Could the information possibly get to the leaders? "I am going to the feast when the right time comes," is what He said. After His family had gone, Jesus went to Jerusalem "undercover," so as not to call attention to Himself.

In our Lord's actions, we see a beautiful illustration of divine sovereignty and human responsibility. The Father had a plan for His Son, and nothing could spoil that plan. Jesus did not tempt the Father by rushing to the feast, nor did He lag behind when the proper time had come for Him to attend the feast. It requires spiritual discernment to know God's timing.

2. In the Midst of the Feast: Debate (7:11–36)

Note that this public debate about the Lord Jesus involved three different groups of people. First, of course, were the Jewish leaders ("the Jews") who lived in Jerusalem and were attached to the temple ministry. This would include the Pharisees and the chief priests (most of whom were Sadducees) as well as the scribes. These men differed theologically, but they agreed on one thing: their opposition to Jesus Christ and their determination to get rid of Him. The exceptions would be Nicodemus and Joseph of Arimathea (John 19:38–42).

The second group would be "the people" (John 7:12, 20, 31–32). This would be the festival crowd that had come to Jerusalem to worship. Many of them would not be influenced by the attitude of the religious leaders at Jerusalem. You will note in John 7:20 that "the people" were amazed that anybody would want to kill Jesus! They were not up to date on all the gossip in the city and had to learn the hard way that Jesus was considered a lawbreaker by the officials.

The third group was composed of the Jews who resided in Jerusalem (John 7:25). They, of course, would have likely sided with the religious leaders.

The debate began before Jesus even arrived at the city, and it centered on *His character* (John 7:11–13). The religious leaders "kept seeking" Jesus, while the crowd kept arguing whether He was a good man or a deceiver. He would have to be one or the other, because a truly good man would not deceive anybody. Yes, Jesus is either what He claims to be, or He is a liar.

But when Jesus began to teach openly in the temple, the debate shifted to *His doctrine* (John 7:14–19). Character and doctrine go together, of course. It would be foolish to trust the teachings of a liar! The Jews were amazed at what He taught because He did not have any credentials from their approved rabbinical schools. But since He lacked this "proper accreditation," His enemies said that His teachings were nothing but private opinions and not worth much. It has often been said that Jesus taught with authority, while the scribes and Pharisees taught from authorities, quoting all the famous rabbis.

Jesus explained that His doctrine came from the Father. He had already made it clear that He and the Father were one in the works that He performed (John 5:17) and in the judgment that He executed (John 5:30). Now He claimed that His teachings also came from the Father, and He would make that astounding claim again (John 8:26, 38). When I teach the Word of God, I can claim authority for the Bible but not for all of my interpretations of the Bible. Jesus rightly could claim absolute authority for everything that He taught!

But does not *every* religious teacher make a similar claim? How, then, can we know that Jesus is teaching us the truth? *By obeying what He tells us to do.* God's Word proves itself true to those who will sincerely do it. The British preacher F. W. Robertson said that "obedience is the organ of spiritual knowledge." John 7:17 literally reads, "If any man is willing to do His [God's] will, he shall know." This explains why the Jewish leaders did not understand Jesus' teachings; they had stubborn wills and would not submit to Him (John 5:40).

Is our Lord suggesting here a "pragmatic test" for divine truth? Is He saying, "Try it! If it works, it must be true!" and thus suggesting that if it does not work it must be false? This kind of a test would lead to confusion, for almost any cultist could say, "I tried what the cult teaches, and it works!"

No, our Lord's statement goes much deeper. He was not suggesting a shallow "taste test" but rather the deep personal commitment of the person to truth. The Jews depended on education and authorities and received their doctrine secondhand, but Jesus insisted that we experience the authority of truth *personally*. The Jewish leaders were attempting to *kill Jesus*, yet at the same time they claimed to understand God's truth and obey it. This proves that an enlightened and educated mind is no guarantee of a pure heart or a sanctified will. Some of the world's worst criminals have been highly intelligent and well-educated people.

Satan offered Adam and Eve knowledge, but it was knowledge based on disobedience (Gen. 3:5). Jesus offered knowledge as the result of obedience: first the yoke of responsibility, then the joy of knowing God's truth. Dr. G. Campbell Morgan said it perfectly: "When men are wholly, completely consecrated to the will of God and want to do that above everything else, then they find out that Christ's teaching is divine, that it is the teaching of God."

If we really seek God's will, then we will not worry over who gets the glory. All truth is God's truth, and God alone deserves the glory for what He has taught us. No teacher or preacher can take the credit for what only can come from God. If he does go after the glory, then it is proof that his teaching is self-generated and not received from God. This is the origin of many cults and church splits: Somebody "invents" a doctrine, takes credit for it, and uses it to divide God's people.

The first "debate" was with the Jews, but the visitors to the city entered into the discussion (John 7:20). Jesus had boldly announced that the leaders wanted to kill Him because He had violated the Sabbath and then claimed to be God (see John 5:10–18). The orthodox Jews broke the Sabbath laws when they had their sons circumcised on the Sabbath, so why could He not heal a man on the Sabbath? "Why go ye about to kill me?"

The visitors, of course, did not know that their leaders were out to kill Jesus, so they challenged His statement. But their reply contained a serious accusation—that Jesus had a demon. This was not a new accusation, for the leaders had said it before (Matt. 9:32ff.; 10:25; 11:18–19; 12:24ff.). "You must be crazy to think that anybody wants to kill You!"

Our Lord used the very law of Moses to refute the enemy's argument, but He knew that they would not give in. Why? Because their standard of judgment was not honest. They evaluated things on the basis of superficial examination of the facts. They judged on the basis of "seems" and not "is." Unfortunately, too many people make that same mistake today. John 7:24 is the opposite of verse 17, where Jesus called for sincere devotion to truth.

The residents of Jerusalem entered the conversation (John 7:25). They knew that the rulers wanted to kill Jesus, and they were amazed that He was teaching openly and getting away with it! Perhaps the rulers had been convinced that indeed He is the Messiah, sent from God! Then why were they not worshipping Him and leading others to worship Him?

Their question (John 7:25) suggested a negative answer: "No, the rulers do not believe that He is the Christ, do they?" They were able to defend their conclusion with logic:

1. Nobody knows where the Christ comes from.

2. We know where Jesus of Nazareth came from.

3. Conclusion: Jesus cannot be the Messiah.

Once again, the people could not see the truth because they were blinded by what they thought were dependable facts. Jesus had met this same kind of resistance in the synagogue in Capernaum (John 6:42ff.). Even the learned teachers—the "expert builders"—would not be able to identify the Chief Cornerstone, even though they had studied the God-given "blueprints" for centuries (Acts 4:11)!

At this point, our Lord raised His voice so that everybody could hear (note also John 7:37). He was probably speaking in a tone revealing irony: "Yes, you think you know Me and where I came from! But really, you do not!" Then He explained why they did not know Him: *They did not know the Father!* This was a serious accusation to make against an orthodox Jew, for the Jews prided themselves in knowing the true God, the God of Israel.

But Jesus went even further: He boldly asserted that He not only knew the Father, but also was sent by Him! He was once again claiming to be God! He was not simply *born* into this world like any other human; He was *sent* to earth by the Father. This means that He existed before He was born on the earth.

This was certainly a crisis hour in His ministry, and some of the leaders tried to have Him arrested, but "his hour was not yet come." Many of the pilgrims put their faith in Him. It was a faith based on miracles, but at least it was a beginning (see John 2:23; 6:2, 26). Nicodemus first became interested in Jesus because of His miracles (John 3:1–2), and eventually he openly professed faith in Christ.

The Pharisees and chief priests, who presided over the Jewish religious establishment, resented the fact that the people were trusting in Jesus. Apparently these "believers" were not afraid to tell what they had done (John 7:13, 32). This time, the rulers sent members of the temple guard to arrest Jesus, but it was Jesus who "arrested" them! He warned them that they had but "a little while" to hear the truth, believe, and be saved (see John 12:35ff.). It was not Jesus who was in danger, but those who wanted to arrest Him!

As in previous messages, the people misunderstood what Jesus was saying. Within six months, Jesus would go back to the Father in heaven, and the unsaved Jews would not be able to follow Him. What a contrast between "where I am, thither ye cannot come" (John 7:34) and "that where I am, there ye may be also" (John 14:3)!

Had these men been willing to do God's will, they would have known the truth. Soon it would be too late.

3. THE END OF THE FEAST: DIVISION (7:37–52)

The last day of the feast would be the seventh day, a very special day on which the priests would march seven times around the altar, chanting

Psalm 118:25, It would be the last time they would draw the water and pour it out. No doubt just as they were pouring out the water, symbolic of the water Moses drew from the rock, Jesus stood and shouted His great invitation to thirsty sinners.

It has been pointed out that this "great day," the twenty-first of the seventh month, is the same date on which the prophet Haggai made a special prediction about the temple (Hag. 2:1–9). While the ultimate fulfillment must await the return of Christ to this earth, certainly there was a partial fulfillment when Jesus came to the temple. Haggai 2:6–7 is quoted in Hebrews 12:26–29 as applying to the return of the Lord.

Jesus was referring to the experience of Israel recorded in Exodus 17:1–7. That water was but a picture of the Spirit of God. Believers would not only drink the living water, but they would become channels of living water to bless a thirsty world! The "artesian well" that He promised in John 4:14 has now become a flowing river! While there are no specific prophetic Scriptures that indicate "rivers of water" flowing from the believer, there are a number of verses that parallel this thought: Isaiah 12:3; 15; 32:2; 44:3; and 58:11; and Zechariah 14:8. Note that Zechariah 14:16ff. speaks about the future Feast of Tabernacles, when the Lord is King.

Water for drinking is one of the symbols of the Holy Spirit in the Bible. (Water for washing is a symbol of the Word of God; see John 15:3; Eph. 5:26.) Just as water satisfies thirst and produces fruitfulness, so the Spirit of God satisfies the inner person and enables us to bear fruit. At the feast, the Jews were reenacting a tradition that could never satisfy the heart. Jesus offered them living water and eternal satisfaction!

What was the result of this declaration and invitation? The people were divided: Some defended Him, and some wanted to arrest Him. Is He a "good man" or "a deceiver" (John 7:12)? Is He "the Christ" (John 7:31)?

Is He the promised "Prophet" (John 7:40; Deut. 18:15)? If only they had honestly examined the evidence, they would have discovered that, indeed, He was the Christ, the Son of God. They identified Jesus with Galilee (John 1:45–46; 7:52) when in reality He was born in Bethlehem (see John 6:42 for similar reasoning).

The temple officers returned to the Jewish council meeting empty-handed. It certainly should have been relatively easy for them to arrest Jesus, yet they failed to do so. What stopped them? "Never man spake like this man!" was their defense. In other words, "This Jesus is more than a man! No mere man speaks as He does!" They were "arrested" by the word of God, spoken by the Son of God.

Again, the leaders refused to face facts honestly but passed judgment on the basis of their prejudices and their superficial examination of the facts. It is much easier to label people (and *libel* people!) than to listen to the facts they present. "So some of the people have believed on Jesus! So what? These common people know nothing about the law anyway! Have any *important* people—like ourselves—believed on Him? Of course not!" They would use a similar argument to try to discredit the witness of the blind man whom Jesus healed (John 9:34).

We should not be surprised when "the intelligentsia" refuses to trust Jesus Christ or when religious leaders reject Him. God has hidden His truth from "the wise and prudent" and revealed it to "spiritual babes," the humble people who will yield to Him (Matt. 11:25–27). Paul was a very intelligent rabbi when God saved him, yet he had to be "knocked down" before he would acknowledge that Jesus Christ was the resurrected Son of God. Read 1 Corinthians 1:26–31 to learn Paul's explanation for the difficulty of winning "smart religious people" to the Savior.

No doubt the rulers would have sent the guard out again, but Nicodemus spoke up. This man is found three times in John's gospel, and each time he is identified as the one "who came to Jesus by night" (see John 3:1–2; 19:39). No doubt Nicodemus had been doing a great deal of thinking and studying since that first interview with Jesus, and he was not afraid to take his stand for truth.

Nicodemus was sure that the council was not giving Jesus an honest hearing. The rulers had already passed judgment and were trying to arrest Him before He had even been given a fair and lawful trial! Perhaps Nicodemus had in mind such Old Testament Scriptures as Exodus 23:1 and Deuteronomy 1:16–17; 19:15–21.

What did Nicodemus want them to consider about Jesus? His words and His works. It was Jesus the Teacher and the miracle worker who had attracted Nicodemus's interest in the first place (John 3:2). In fact, Jesus had pointed to His works as proof of His deity (John 5:32), and He repeatedly urged the people to pay attention to His words. The two go together, for the miracles point to the messages, and the messages interpret the spiritual meaning of the miracles.

You can hear the sarcasm and disdain in the reply of the rulers: "Are you a lowly and despised Galilean too?" They refused to admit that Nicodemus was right in asking for a fair trial, but the only way they could answer him was by means of ridicule. This is an ancient debate trick: When you cannot answer the argument, attack the speaker.

They challenged Nicodemus to search the prophecies to see if he could find any statement that a prophet would come out of Galilee. Of course, Jonah was from Galilee, and Jesus said that Jonah was a picture of Himself in death, burial, and resurrection (Matt. 12:38–41). Perhaps Nicodemus read Isaiah 9:1–2 (see Matt. 4:12–16) and began to trace the great messianic prophecies in the Old Testament. If he did, then he became convinced that Jesus of Nazareth was the very Son of God.

You cannot help but feel sorry for the people described in this chapter, people who responded to Jesus in the wrong ways. His half brothers responded with disbelief, various people responded with debate, and the result was division. Had they willingly received the truth, and had they acted with sincere obedience, they would have ended up at the feet of Jesus, confessing Him as Messiah and Son of God.

But people *today* commit the same blunder and permit their prejudices and superficial evaluations to blind them to the truth.

Don't let it happen to you!

QUESTIONS FOR PERSONAL REFLECTION
OR GROUP DISCUSSION

1. When have you shared the gospel with someone who was offended? Why do you think that person reacted as he or she did?

2. Read verses 1–10. How did Jesus' half brothers respond to Him and His teaching?

3. What did Jesus mean when He said, "My time is not yet fully come"?

4. Read verses 11–52. What were Jesus' main teaching points about Himself?

5. What evidence or experience convinces you that Jesus really was sent from God?

6. What are we to make of the fact that many people look at that same evidence and find it unconvincing?

7. What was significant about Jesus' invitation in verses 37–39?

8. How does a person "drink" what Jesus is offering?

9. Read verse 17. Has obedience to Christ demonstrated to you that He is who He is? If so, in what way?

10. How can you motivate yourself to witness to people even though they may become offended?

Chapter Eight

CONTRASTS AND CONFLICTS

(John 8)

Is the story of the woman taken in adultery a part of Scripture? If it is, where does it belong in the gospel record? John 7:53—8:11 is not found in some of the ancient manuscripts; where it is found, it is not always in this location in John's gospel. Most scholars seem to agree that the passage is a part of inspired Scripture ("a fragment of authentic gospel material," says Dr. F. F. Bruce) regardless of where it is placed.

To many of us, the story fits right here! In fact, the development of the entire chapter can easily be seen to grow out of this striking event in the temple. Our Lord's declaration on His being the Light of the World (John 8:12) certainly fits, and so do His words about true and false judgment (John 8:15–16, 26). The repeated phrase "die in your sins" (John 8:21, 24) would clearly relate to the judgment of the woman, and the fact that the chapter ends with an attempt to stone Jesus shows a perfect parallel to the opening story. The transition from John 7:52 to 8:12 would be too abrupt without a transitional section.

Our Lord found Himself again in conflict with the Jewish religious leaders, but this time, they set a trap, hoping to get enough evidence to arrest Jesus and get Him out of the way. However, their plot failed, but a controversy followed. In this chapter we see a series of contrasts that reveal the graciousness of Christ and the wickedness of people.

Grace and Law (8:1–11)

The Feast of Tabernacles had ended, but Jesus took advantage of the opportunity to minister to the pilgrims in the temple. During the feast, word had quickly spread that Jesus was not only attending but also openly teaching in the temple (see Luke 21:37). He taught in the court of the women at the place where the treasury was situated (John 8:20). The scribes and Pharisees knew where He would be, so they hatched their plot together.

They would not be likely to catch a couple in the "very act" of adultery, so we wonder if the man (who never was indicted!) was part of the scheme. The law required that *both* guilty parties be stoned (Lev. 20:10; Deut. 22:22) and not just the woman. It does seem suspicious that the man went free. The scribes and Pharisees handled the matter in a brutal fashion, even in the way they interrupted the Lord's teaching and pushed the woman into the midst of the crowd.

The Jewish leaders, of course, were trying to pin Jesus on the horns of a dilemma. If He said, "Yes, the woman must be stoned!" then what would happen to His reputation as the "friend of publicans and sinners"? The common people would no doubt have abandoned Him and would never have accepted His gracious message of forgiveness.

But, if He said, "No, the woman should not be stoned!" then He was openly breaking the law and subject to arrest. On more than one occasion, the religious leaders had tried to pit Jesus against Moses, and now they seemed to have the perfect challenge (see John 5:39–47; 6:32ff.; 7:40ff.).

Instead of passing judgment on the woman, Jesus passed judgment on the judges! No doubt He was indignant at the way they treated the woman. He was also concerned that such hypocrites should condemn another person and not judge themselves. We do not know what He wrote on the dirt floor of the temple. Was He simply reminding them that the Ten Commandments had been originally written "with the finger of God" (Ex. 31:18) and that He is God? Or was He perhaps reminding them of the warning in Jeremiah 17:13?

It was required by Jewish law that the accusers cast the first stones (Deut. 17:7). Jesus was not asking that sinless men judge the woman, for He was the only sinless Person present. If our judges today had to be perfect, judicial benches would be empty. He was referring to *the particular sin of the woman,* a sin that can be committed in the heart as well as with the body (Matt. 5:27–30). Convicted by their own consciences, the accusers quietly left the scene, and Jesus was left alone with the woman. He forgave her and warned her to sin no more (John 5:14).

We must not misinterpret this event to mean that Jesus was "easy on sin" or that He contradicted the law. For Jesus to forgive this woman meant that He had to one day die for her sins. Forgiveness is free, but it is not cheap. Furthermore, Jesus perfectly fulfilled the law so that no one could justly accuse Him of opposing its teachings or weakening its power. By applying the law to the woman *and not to themselves,* the Jewish leaders were violating both the letter and the spirit of the law—and they thought they were defending Moses!

The law was given to reveal sin (Rom. 3:20), and we must be condemned by the law before we can be cleansed by God's grace. Law and grace do not compete with each other; they complement each other. Nobody was ever saved by keeping the law, but nobody was ever saved by grace who was not *first* indicted by the law. There must be conviction before there can be conversion.

Nor is Christ's gracious forgiveness an excuse to sin. "Go, and sin no more!" was our Lord's counsel. "But there is forgiveness with thee, that thou mayest be feared" (Ps. 130:4). Certainly the experience of gracious forgiveness would motivate the penitent sinner to live a holy and obedient life to the glory of God.

LIGHT AND DARKNESS (8:12–20)

This second great "I am" statement certainly fits into the context of the first eleven verses of John 8. Perhaps the sun was then appearing (John 8:2) so that Jesus was comparing Himself to the rising sun. But this would mean He was once again claiming to be God, for to the Jew, the sun was a symbol of Jehovah God (Ps. 84:11; Mal. 4:2). There is, for our galaxy, only one sun, and it is the center and the source of life. So there is but one God who is the center of all and the source of all life (John 1:4). "God is light" (1 John 1:5), and wherever the light shines, it reveals humanity's wickedness (Eph. 5:8–14).

Our Lord's "I am" statement was also related to the Feast of Tabernacles, during which the huge candelabra were lit in the temple at night to remind the people of the pillar of fire that had guided Israel in its wilderness journey. In fact, John has combined three "wilderness images": the manna (John 6), the water from the rock (John 7), and the pillar of fire (John 8).

To "follow" the Lord Jesus means to believe in Him, to trust Him, and the results are *life* and *light* for the believer. The unsaved are walking in darkness because they love darkness (John 3:17ff.). One of the major messages in this gospel is that the spiritual light is now shining, but people cannot comprehend it—and they try to put it out (John 1:4–5).

Not all of the Jewish leaders had left the group, and others had no doubt come along after the woman left. As usual, they debated with Jesus. This time, they accused Him of bearing witness to Himself by claiming to be the Light of the World, and Jewish courts would not permit a person to bear witness to himself.

But light *has to* bear witness to itself! The only people who cannot see the light are *blind* people!

I recall the first time I flew at night. I was fascinated by the changing textures of colored lights in the cities below me. When our plane left the New York area and headed out into the night, I was amazed that I could see pinpoints of light miles away. Then I understood why it was necessary to have blackouts during the war, for the enemy pilots could see the smallest evidence of light and thus find the target. Light bears witness to itself; it tells you it is there.

Perhaps the Pharisees were quoting our Lord's own words (see John 5:31ff.), but He quickly refuted *their* argument. One of the key words in this section is *witness;* it is used seven times. Jesus made it clear that their witness was not dependable because their judgment was faulty. They judged on the basis of externals, mere human judgment, but He judged on the basis of spiritual knowledge. The way they judged the woman taken in adultery proved that they understood neither the law nor their own sinful hearts.

Since they wanted to use the law to condemn the woman and trap the Savior, Jesus also used the law to answer them. He quoted a principle found in Deuteronomy 17:6 and 19:15, as well as Numbers 35:30, that the testimony of two men was required to validate a judgment. Jesus had those two testimonies: *He* gave witness and so did *His Father.* We have seen from John 5:37–47 that the witness of the Father is found in the Word of God.

How tragic that these experts in the law did not even know their own Messiah as He stood before them! They claimed to know the law of God, but they did not know the God of the law. They did not have His

Word abiding in their hearts (John 5:38), nor did they experience His love (John 5:42). They did not know the Father and therefore did not know the Son.

Jesus never really answered their question, "Where is thy Father?" The word *father* is used twenty-one times in this chapter, so Jesus did not avoid the issue but faced it honestly. He knew that their "father" was not God— but the Devil! These men were religious, and yet they were the children of the Devil!

Their further attempts to arrest Jesus were again thwarted by the Father, for it was not yet our Lord's hour when He should give His life. When the servants of God are in the will of God, they can have courage and peace as they does their duty.

LIFE AND DEATH (8:21–30)

Jesus had already mentioned His leaving them (John 7:34), but the Jews had misunderstood what He said. Once again, He warned them: He would leave them, they would not be able to follow Him, and they would die in their sins! They were wasting their God-given opportunities by arguing with Him instead of trusting Him, and one day soon, their opportunities would end.

Once again, the people misunderstood His teaching. They thought He was planning to kill Himself! Suicide was an abhorrent thing to a Jew, for the Jews were taught to honor all life. If Jesus committed suicide, then He would go to a place of judgment, and this, they reasoned, was why they could not follow Him.

Actually, just the opposite was true: It was *they* who were going to the place of judgment! Jesus was returning to His Father in heaven, and nobody can go there who has not trusted the Savior. The reason Jesus and the Jewish leaders were going to different destinations was because they had different *origins:* Jesus came from heaven, but they belonged to the earth. Jesus was *in* the world, but He did not belong to the world (see John 17:14–16).

The true believer has his citizenship in heaven (Luke 10:20; Phil. 3:20–21). His affection and attention are fixed heavenward. But the unsaved belong to this world; in fact, Jesus called them "the children of this world" (Luke 16:8). Since they have not trusted Christ and had their sins forgiven, their destiny is to die in their sins. The Christian dies "in the Lord" because he lives "in the Lord" (Rev. 14:13), but the unbeliever dies in his sins because he lives in his sins.

It seems incredible that these religious "experts" should ask, "Who are You?" He had given them every evidence that He is the Son of God, yet they had deliberately rejected the evidence. Our Lord's reply may be expressed, "I am exactly what I said!" In other words, "Why should I teach you *new* things, or give you *new* proof, when you have not honestly considered the witness I have already given?"

Jesus boldly made several claims to deity (John 8:26). He said He would judge, and judgment (to the Jews) belonged only to God. He claimed to be sent by God, and He claimed to have heard from God the things that He taught. How did the religious leaders respond to these clear affirmations of deity? They did not understand! God reveals His truth to the "babes" and not to the "wise and prudent" (Luke 10:21).

Now Jesus spoke about His own death, when He would be "lifted up" on the cross (John 3:14; 12:32). The word translated "lifted up" has a dual meaning: "lifted up in crucifixion" and "lifted up in exaltation and glorification." Jesus often combined the two, for He saw His crucifixion in terms of glory and not just suffering (John 12:23; 13:30–31; 17:1). This same combination of "suffering and glory" is repeated in Peter's first letter.

It would be in His death, burial, resurrection, and ascension that Jesus would be revealed to the Jewish nation. This was the message Peter preached at Pentecost (Acts 2), not only the death of Jesus but also His resurrection and exaltation to glory. Even a Roman soldier, beholding the events at Golgotha would confess, "Truly this man was the Son of God" (Mark 15:39). The early church, following the example of its Lord (Luke 24:25–27), would show from the Old Testament prophecies both the sufferings and the glory of the Messiah.

Jesus made two more stupendous claims: Not only was He sent by the Father, but the Father was with Him because He always did what pleased the Father (John 8:29). No doubt, His enemies reacted violently to these words, but some of the listeners put their faith in Him. Whether this was true saving faith or not (see John 2:23–25), we cannot tell, but our Lord's words to them would indicate that they knew what they were doing.

Salvation is a matter of life or death. People who live in their sins and reject the Savior must die in their sins. There is no alternative. We either receive salvation by grace or experience condemnation under God's law. We either walk in the light and have eternal life, or walk in the darkness and experience eternal death. There is a fourth contrast.

Freedom and Bondage (8:31–47)

What listeners are represented by the pronoun *they* in John 8:33? In the previous verses, Jesus addressed the "believers" mentioned in John 8:30, and He warned them that continuance in the Word—discipleship—was proof of true salvation. When we obey His Word, we grow in spiritual knowledge, and as we grow in spiritual knowledge, we grow in freedom from sin. Life leads to learning, and learning leads to liberty.

It is not likely that the pronoun *they* refers to these new believers, for they would probably not argue with their Savior! If John 8:37 is any guide, "they" probably refers to the same unbelieving Jewish leaders who had opposed Jesus throughout this conversation (John 8:13, 19, 22, 25). As before, they did not understand His message. Jesus was speaking about true spiritual freedom, freedom from sin, but they were thinking about political freedom.

Their claim that Abraham's descendants had never been in bondage was certainly a false one that was refuted by the very record in the Old Testament Scriptures. The Jews had been enslaved by seven mighty nations, as recorded in the book of Judges. The ten northern tribes had been carried away captive by Assyria, and the two southern tribes had gone into seventy years of captivity in Babylon. And at that very hour, the Jews were under the iron heel of Rome! How difficult it is for proud religious people to admit their failings and their needs!

Jesus explained that the difference between spiritual freedom and bondage is a matter of whether one is a son or a servant. The servant may live in the house, but he is not a part of the family, and he cannot be guaranteed a future. (Jesus may have had Isaac and Ishmael in mind here; see Gen. 21.) "Whosoever keeps on practicing sin [literal translation] is the servant of sin." These religious leaders would not only *die* in their sins (John 8:21, 24), but they were right then *living* in bondage to sin!

How can slaves of sin be set free? Only by the Son. How does He do it? Through the power of His Word. Note the emphasis on the Word in John 8:38–47, and He had already told them, "The truth shall make you free" (John 8:32). They would not "make room" for His Word in their hearts.

In the rest of this section, you see the debate centering around the word *father*. Jesus identified Himself with the Father in heaven, but He identified them with the father from hell, Satan. Of course, the Jews claimed Abraham as their father (Luke 3:8ff.), but Jesus made a careful distinction between "Abraham's seed" (physical descendants) and "Abraham's children" (spiritual descendants because of personal faith; Gal. 3:6–14).

These Jewish leaders, who claimed to belong to Abraham, were very unlike Abraham. For one thing, they wanted to kill Jesus; Abraham was the "friend of God" and fellowshipped with Him in love (Isa. 41:8). Abraham listened to God's truth and obeyed it, but these religious leaders rejected the truth.

Nature is determined by birth, and birth is determined by paternity. If God is your Father, then you share God's nature (2 Peter 1:1–4), but if Satan is your father, then you share in his evil nature. Our Lord did not say that *every* lost sinner is a "child of the devil," though every lost sinner is certainly a child of wrath and disobedience (Eph. 2:1–3). Both here and in the parable of the tares (Matt. 13:24–30, 36–43), Jesus said that the Pharisees and other "counterfeit" believers were the children of the Devil. Satan is an imitator (2 Cor. 11:13–15), and he gives his children a false righteousness that can never gain them entrance into heaven (Rom. 10:1–4).

What were the characteristics of these religious leaders who belonged to the Devil? For one thing, they rejected the truth (John 8:40) and tried to kill Jesus because He spoke the truth. They did not love God (John 8:42), nor could they understand what Jesus taught (John 8:43, 47). Satan's children may be well versed in their religious traditions, but they have no understanding of the Word of God.

Satan is a liar and a murderer. He lied to our first parents ("Yea, hath God said …?") and engineered their deaths. Cain was a child of the Devil (1 John 3:12), for he was both a liar and a murderer. He killed his brother Abel and then lied about it (Gen. 4). Is it any wonder that these religious leaders lied about Jesus, hired false witnesses, and then had Him killed?

The worst bondage is the kind that the prisoner himself does not recognize. He thinks he is free, yet he is really a slave. The Pharisees and other religious leaders thought that they were free, but they were actually enslaved in terrible spiritual bondage to sin and Satan. They would not face the truth, and yet it was the truth alone that could set them free.

HONOR AND DISHONOR (8:48–59)

The leaders could not refute our Lord's statements, so they attacked His person. Some students think that the leaders' statement in John 8:41—"We [are] not born of fornication"—was a slur on our Lord's own birth and character. After all, Mary was with child before she and Joseph were married. But the personal attacks in John 8:48 are quite obvious. For a Jew to be called a Samaritan was the grossest of insults, and then to be called a demon-possessed person only added further insult.

Note that Jesus did not even dignify the racial slur with an answer. (No doubt there was also in this the suggestion that, like the Samaritans, Jesus was a heretic.) They were dishonoring Him, but He was honoring the Father. You will recall that He made it clear that it was impossible to honor the Father without honoring the Son (John 5:23). They were seeking their own glory (see John 5:41–44), but He was seeking the glory that belongs to God alone. Tradition-centered religion, without Christ, is often a "mutual admiration society" for people who want the praise of other people.

Jesus had warned them that they would die in their sins because of their unbelief, and now He invited them to trust His Word and "never see death" (John 8:51). He had said this before in His synagogue sermon (John 6:39–40, 44, 54). Once again, the leaders lacked the spiritual insight to understand what He was saying. Abraham was dead, yet he was a godly man, and the faithful prophets were also dead. This kind of talk only convinced them the more that He had a demon (John 7:20)!

By claiming to be the Lord of death, He was claiming to be God (John 5:21–29). This was not an honor He made for Himself; the Father gave it to Him. In fact, Abraham (whom they claimed as their father) saw His day and rejoiced! Instead of rejoicing, they were revolting and trying to kill Him.

How did Abraham "see" our Lord's day, that is, His life and ministry on earth? The same way he saw the future city: by faith (Heb. 11:10, 13–16). God did not give Abraham some special vision of our Lord's life and ministry, but He did give him the spiritual perception to "see" these future events. Certainly Abraham saw the birth of the Messiah in the miraculous birth of his own son, Isaac. He certainly saw Calvary when he offered Isaac to God (Gen. 22). In the priestly ministry of Melchizedek (Gen. 14:17–24), Abraham could see the heavenly priesthood of the Lord. In the marriage of Isaac, Abraham could see a picture of the marriage of the Lamb (Gen. 24).

His statement found in John 8:58 can be translated, "Before Abraham came into being, I Am." Again, this was another affirmation of His divine sonship, and the Jewish leaders received it as such. He had once again made Himself equal with God (John 5:18), and this was the sin of blasphemy, worthy of death (Lev. 24:16). Jesus was divinely protected and simply walked away. His hour had not yet come. We cannot help but admire His courage as He presented the truth and invited blind religious men to trust Him and be set free.

The most difficult people to win to the Savior are those who do not realize that they have a need. They are under the condemnation of God, yet they trust their religion to save them. They are walking in the darkness and not following the Light of Life. They are sharing a "living death" because of their bondage to sin; and, in spite of their religious deeds, they are dishonoring the Father and the Son. These are the people who crucified Jesus Christ, and Jesus called them the children of the Devil.

Whose child are you? Is God your Father because you have received Jesus Christ into your life (John 1:12–13)? Or is Satan your father because you are depending on a counterfeit righteousness, a "works righteousness," not the righteousness that comes through faith in Jesus Christ?

If God is your Father, then heaven is your home. If He is not your Father, then hell is your destiny.

It is truly a matter of life or death!

QUESTIONS FOR PERSONAL REFLECTION
OR GROUP DISCUSSION

1. What are some common objections to Christianity?

2. Read verses 1–11. What trap were the Pharisees trying to catch Jesus in?

3. Why did Jesus let the adulterous woman go?

4. What attitudes toward sin—your own sin and others' sin—does this story encourage you to learn from Jesus?

5. Read verses 12–20. What did Jesus mean when He said, "I am the light of the world"?

6. What was Jesus' main point in this argument with the Pharisees?

7. Read verses 21–30. What claims to deity did Jesus make?

8. Why does it matter that Jesus claimed to be God?

9. Why do many people find this claim so offensive?

10. Read verses 31–59. What did Jesus teach about freedom and bondage?

11. When have you (or people you know) resisted facing the truth that you (or they) were in bondage?

12. How do you think God wants you to interact with people who reject what Jesus said about Himself and about them?

Chapter Nine

THE BLIND MAN CALLS THEIR BLUFF

(John 9)

Our Lord performed miracles in order to meet human needs. But He also used those miracles as a "launching pad" for a message conveying spiritual truth. Finally, His miracles were His "credentials" to prove that He was indeed the Messiah. "The blind receive their sight" was one such messianic miracle (Matt. 11:5), and we see it demonstrated in this chapter. Jesus used this miracle as the basis for a short sermon on spiritual blindness (John 9:39–41) and a longer sermon on true and false shepherds (John 10:1–18).

I am told that in the United States somebody goes blind every twenty minutes. The man we meet in this chapter was *born* blind; he had never seen the beauty of God's creation or the faces of his loved ones. When Jesus arrived on the scene, everything changed, and the man was made to see. However, the greatest miracle was not the opening of his eyes but the opening of his heart to the Savior. It cost him everything to confess Jesus as the Son of God, but he was willing to do it.

The easiest way to grasp the message of this chapter is to note the stages in this man's growing understanding of who Jesus is.

"A Man Called" (9:1–12)

About the only thing a blind man could do in that day was beg, and that is what this man was doing when Jesus passed by (John 9:8). No doubt there were many blind people who would have rejoiced to be healed, but Jesus selected this man (see Luke 4:25–27). Apparently the man and his parents were well known in the community. It was on the Sabbath when Jesus healed the man (John 9:14), so that once again He was upsetting and deliberately challenging the religious leaders (John 5:9ff.).

The disciples did not look at the man as an object of mercy but rather as a subject for a theological discussion. It is much easier to discuss an abstract subject like "sin" than it is to minister to a concrete need in the life of a person. The disciples were sure that the man's congenital blindness was caused by sin, either his own or his parents', but Jesus disagreed with them.

In the final analysis, *all* physical problems are the result of our fall in Adam, for his disobedience brought sin and death into the world (Rom. 5:12ff.). But afterward, to blame a specific disability on a specific sin committed by specific persons is certainly beyond any person's ability or authority. Only God knows why babies are born with disabilities, and only God can turn those disabilities into something that will bring good to the people and glory to His name.

Certainly both the man and his parents had at some time committed sin, but Jesus did not see their sin as the cause of the man's blindness. Nor did He suggest that God deliberately made the man blind so that, years later, Jesus could perform a miracle. Since there is no punctuation in the original manuscripts, we are free to read John 9:3–4 this way: "Neither has this man sinned nor his parents. But that the works of God should be made manifest in him, I must work the works of Him who sent Me, while it is day."

Our Lord's method of healing was unique: He put clay on the man's eyes and told him to go and wash. Once Jesus healed two blind men by merely touching their eyes (Matt. 9:27–31), and He healed another blind man by putting spittle on his eyes (Mark 8:22–26). Though the healing power was the same, our Lord varied His methods lest people focus on the *manner* of healing and miss the *message* in the healing.

There were at least two reasons for our Lord's use of the clay. For one thing, it was a picture of the *incarnation*. God made the first man out of the dust, and God sent His Son as a real Man. Note the emphasis on the meaning of "Siloam"—"sent." And relate this to John 9:4: "The works of him that sent me" (see also John 3:17, 34; 5:36; 7:29; 8:18, 42). Jesus gave a little illustration of His own coming to earth, sent by the Father.

The second reason for the clay was *irritation;* it encouraged the man to believe and obey! If you have ever had an irritation in your eyes, you know how quickly you seek *irrigation* to cleanse it out! You might compare this "irritation" to the convicting work of the Holy Spirit as He uses God's law to bring the lost sinner under judgment.

But the illumination now led to a problem in *identification*: Was this really the blind beggar, and who caused him to see? Throughout the rest of John 9, a growing conflict takes place around these two questions. The religious leaders did not want to face the fact that Jesus had healed the man or even that the man had been healed!

Four times in this chapter people asked, "How were you healed?" (John 9:10, 15, 19, 26). First, the neighbors asked the man, and then the Pharisees asked him. Not satisfied with his reply, the Pharisees then asked the man's parents and then gave the son one final interrogation. All of this looked very official and efficient, but it was really a most evasive maneuver on the part of both the people and the leaders. The Pharisees wanted to get rid of the evidence, and the people were afraid to speak the truth!

They were all asking the wrong question! They should not have asked, "How?" but "Who?" (Simply rearrange the letters!) But we are so prone to ask, "How?" We want to understand the mechanics of a miracle instead of simply trusting the Savior, who alone can perform the miracle. Nicodemus wanted to know how he could reenter his mother's womb (John 3:4, 9). "How can this man give us his flesh to eat?" (John 6:52). Understanding the process, even if we could, is no guarantee that we have experienced the miracle.

When asked to describe his experience, the man simply told what had happened. All he knew about the person who had done the miracle was that He was "a man called Jesus." He had not seen our Lord, of course, but he had heard His voice. Not only was the beggar ignorant of Jesus' identity, but he did not know where Jesus had gone. At this point, the man has been healed, but he has not been saved. The light had dawned, but it would grow brighter until he saw the face of the Lord and worshipped Him (see Prov. 4:18).

At least twelve times in the gospel of John, Jesus is called "a man" (see John 4:29; 5:12; 8:40; 9:11, 24; 10:33; 11:47, 50; 18:14, 17, 29; 19:5). John's emphasis is that Jesus Christ is God, but the apostle balances it beautifully by reminding us that Jesus is also true man. The incarnation was not an illusion (1 John 1:1–4).

"A Prophet" (9:13–23)

Since the Pharisees were the custodians of the faith, it was right that the healed man be brought to them for investigation. The fact that they studied this miracle in such detail is only further proof that Jesus did indeed heal the man. Since the man was *born* blind, the miracle was even greater, for blindness caused by sickness or injury might suddenly go away. Our Lord's miracles can bear careful scrutiny by His enemies.

But Jesus' act of deliberately healing the man on the Sabbath day caused the Pharisees great concern. It was illegal to work on the Sabbath; and by making the clay, applying the clay, and healing the man, Jesus had performed three unlawful "works." The Pharisees should have been praising God for a miracle; instead, they sought evidence to prosecute Jesus.

When people refuse to face evidence honestly, but in fear evade the issue (see John 9:22), then it is impossible to come to a united conclusion. Once again, Jesus was the cause of division (John 9:16; see also 7:12, 43). The religious leaders were judging on the basis of one thing: Nobody who breaks the Sabbath could possibly be a true prophet of God. They were "one-issue" thinkers, not unlike some religious people today. The Pharisees did not realize that Jesus was offering the people something greater than the Sabbath—the true spiritual rest that comes from God (Matt. 11:28–30).

But the beggar was not intimidated by the threats of the Pharisees. When asked who he thought Jesus was, the man boldly said, "He is a prophet!" (Note John 4:19 for a parallel.) Some of the Old Testament prophets, such as Moses, Elijah, and Elisha, did perform miracles. The Jewish people would look on their prophets as men of God who could do wonderful things by the power of God.

But the religious leaders did not want to see Jesus given that kind of high designation. "This man is not of God" (John 9:16). Perhaps they could discredit the miracle. If so, then they could convince the people that Jesus had plotted the whole thing and was really deceiving the people. He had craftily "switched" beggars so that the sighted man was not the man who had been known as the blind beggar.

The best way to get that kind of evidence would be to interrogate the parents of the beggar, so they called them in and asked them two questions: (1) "Is this your son?" and (2) "If he is, how does he now see?" If they refused to answer either question, they were in trouble, or if they answered with replies contrary to what the leaders wanted, they were in trouble. What a dilemma!

They answered the first question honestly: He was their son, and he had been born blind. They answered the second question evasively: They did not know how he was healed or who healed him. They then used the old-fashioned tactic called "passing the buck" by suggesting that the Pharisees ask the man himself. After all, he was of age!

What lay behind all of this questioning and these furtive replies? *The fear of people.* We met it at the Feast of Tabernacles (John 7:13), and we shall meet it again at our Lord's last Passover (John 12:42). These people were seeking the honor of people and not the honor that comes from God (John 5:44). To be sure, it was a serious thing to be excommunicated from the synagogue, but it was far more serious to reject the truth and be lost forever. "The fear of man brings a snare" (Prov. 29:25 NASB). The Pharisees were trying to trap Jesus, and the parents were trying to avoid a trap, but all of them were only ensnaring themselves! The parents should have heeded the counsel of Isaiah 51:7 and 12.

The Pharisees could present a "good case" for their position. After all, they did have the law of Moses as well as centuries of Jewish tradition. What they failed to understand was that Jesus Christ had fulfilled all of this ceremonial law and was now bringing in something new. In Moses, you have preparation, but in Jesus Christ, you have consummation (see John 1:17).

"A Man of God" (9:24–34)

Anxious to settle the case, the Pharisees did call the man in, and this time, they put him under oath. "Give God the praise" is a form of Jewish "swearing in" at court (see Josh. 7:19).

But the "judges" prejudiced everybody from the start! "We know that this man is a sinner!" They were warning the witness that he had better cooperate with the court, or he might be excommunicated. But the beggar was made of sturdier stuff than to be intimidated. He had experienced a miracle, and he was not afraid to tell them what had happened.

He did not debate the character of Jesus Christ, because that was beyond his knowledge and experience. But one thing he did know: Now he could see. His testimony (John 9:25) reminds me of Psalm 27. Read that psalm in the light of this chapter, from the viewpoint of the healed beggar, and see how meaningful it becomes.

For the fourth time, the question is asked, "How did He open your eyes?" (see John 9:10, 15, 19, and 26). I can imagine the man getting quite impatient at this point. After all, he had been blind all his life, and there was so much now to see. He certainly did not want to spend much longer in a synagogue court, looking at angry faces and answering the same questions!

We admire the boldness of the man in asking those irate Pharisees if they wanted to follow Jesus! The man expected a negative answer, but he was courageous even to ask it. Unable to refute the evidence, the judges began to revile the witness, and once again Moses is brought into the picture (John 5:46). The Pharisees were cautious men who would consider themselves conservatives, when in reality they were "preservatives." A true conservative takes the best of the past and uses it, but he is also aware of the new things that God is doing. The new grows out of the old (Matt. 13:52). A "preservative" simply embalms the past and preserves it. He is against change and resists the new things that God is doing. Had the Pharisees really understood Moses, they would have known who Jesus was and what He was doing.

The leaders were sure about Moses, but they were not sure about Jesus. They did not know where He came from. He had already told them that He had come from heaven, sent by the Father (John 6:33, 38, 41–42, 50–51). They were sure that He was the natural son of Mary and Joseph and that He was from the city of Nazareth (John 6:42; 7:41–42). They were judging "after the flesh" (John 8:15) and not exercising spiritual discernment.

It seemed incredible to the healed man that the Pharisees would not know this Man who had opened his eyes! How many people were going around Jerusalem, opening the eyes of blind people? Instead of investigating the miracle, these religious leaders should have been investigating the One who did the miracle and learning from Him. The "experts" were rejecting the Stone that was sent to them (Acts 4:11).

The beggar then gave the "experts" a lesson in practical theology. Perhaps he had Psalm 66:18 in mind: "If I regard iniquity in my heart, the Lord will not hear me." The leaders called Jesus a sinner (John 9:24), yet Jesus was used of God to open the blind man's eyes.

He added another telling argument: Jesus healed a man *born* blind. Never, to their knowledge, had this occurred before. So, God not only heard Jesus, but He enabled Him to give the man sight. How, then, could Jesus be a sinner?

Religious bigots do not want to face either evidence or logic. Their minds are made up. Had the Pharisees honestly considered the facts, they would have seen that Jesus is the Son of God, and they could have trusted Him and been saved.

Again, the leaders reviled the man and told him he was born in sin. However, he would not *die* in his sins (see John 8:21, 24); because before this chapter ends, the beggar will come to faith in Jesus Christ. All of us are born in sin (Ps. 51:5), but we need not live in sin (Col. 3:6–7) or die in our sins. Faith in Jesus Christ redeems us from sin and gives us a life of joyful liberty.

The religious leaders officially excommunicated this man from the local synagogue. This meant that the man was cut off from friends and family and looked on by the Jews as a "publican and sinner." But Jesus came for the "outcasts" and never let them down.

"THE SON OF GOD" (9:35–41)

The Good Shepherd always cares for His sheep. Jesus knew that the man had been excommunicated, so He found him and revealed Himself to him. Remember, the man knew our Lord's voice, but he had never seen His face.

The man now reached the climax of his knowledge of Jesus Christ and his faith in Him. It is not enough to believe that He is "a man called Jesus" or even "a prophet" or "a man of God." "Whosoever believeth that Jesus is the Christ is born of God" (1 John 5:1). John wrote his gospel to prove that Jesus is the Son of God and to present to his readers the testimonies of people who met Jesus and affirmed that He is God's Son. This beggar is one such witness.

Jesus identified Himself as the Son of God (see John 9:35; also 5:25), and the beggar believed and was saved (John 9:38). "My sheep hear my voice" (John 10:27). He did not "see and believe"; he *heard* and believed. Not only did he trust the Savior, but he worshipped Him. If Jesus Christ is not God, then why did He accept worship? Peter, Paul, and Barnabas certainly didn't accept worship (see Acts 10:25–26; 14:11–15).

John the Baptist affirmed that Jesus is the Son of God (John 1:34), and so did Nathanael (John 1:49). Jesus stated that He is the Son of God (John 5:25; 9:35), and Peter also affirmed it (John 6:69). Now the healed blind beggar has joined this group of witnesses.

Wherever Jesus went, some of the Pharisees tried to be present so they could catch Him in something He said or did. Seeing them, Jesus closed this episode by preaching a brief but penetrating sermon on spiritual blindness.

John 9:39 does not contradict John 3:16–17. The *reason* for our Lord's coming was salvation, but the *result* of His coming was condemnation of those who would not believe. The same sun that brings beauty out of the seeds also exposes the vermin hiding under the rocks. The religious leaders were blind and would not admit it; therefore, the light of truth only made them blinder. The beggar admitted his need, and he received both physical sight and spiritual sight. No one is so blind as he who will not see, the one who thinks he has "all truth" and there is nothing more for him to learn (John 9:28, 34).

The listening Pharisees heard what Jesus said, and it disturbed them. "Are we blind also?" they asked, expecting a negative answer. Jesus had already called them "blind leaders of the blind" (Matt. 15:14), so they had their answer. They were blinded by their pride, their self-righteousness, their tradition, and their false interpretation of the Word of God.

Our Lord's reply was a paradox. "If you were blind, you would be better off. But you claim to see. Therefore, you are guilty!" Blindness would at least be an excuse for not knowing what was going on. But they *did* know what was going on. Jesus had performed many miracles, and the religious leaders ignored the evidence to make a right decision.

Jesus is the Light of the World (John 8:12; 9:5). The only people who cannot see the light are blind people and those who refuse to look, those who make themselves blind. The beggar was physically blind and spiritually blind, yet both his eyes and his heart were opened. Why? Because he listened to the Word, believed it, obeyed, and experienced the grace of God. The Pharisees had good physical vision, but they were blind spiritually. Had they listened to the Word and sincerely considered the evidence, they too would have believed on Jesus Christ and been born again.

In what sense did the Pharisees "see"? They saw the change in the blind beggar and could not deny that he had been healed. They saw the mighty works that Jesus performed. Even Nicodemus, one of their number, was impressed with the Lord's miracles (John 3:2). If they had examined the evidence with honesty, they would have seen the truth clearly. "If any man wills to do His [God's] will, he shall know of the doctrine" (John 7:17, literal translation). "And ye will not come to me, that ye might have life" (John 5:40).

John 10 is actually a continuation of our Lord's ministry to the Pharisees. The healing of the blind beggar is the background (John 10:21). In fact, the word translated "cast out" in John 9:35 is translated "puts forth" in John 10:4. The beggar was cast out of the synagogue but taken by the Good Shepherd and added to His flock! The emphasis in John 10 is on Jesus Christ, the Good and True Shepherd, as opposed to the Pharisees, who were false shepherds.

We never meet this healed beggar again, but surely the man followed Jesus closely and was among those who witnessed for Him. We hope that he was able to win his fearful parents to the Lord. While being excommunicated from the synagogue was certainly a painful experience for him, he certainly found in his fellowship with Jesus Christ much more spiritual help and encouragement than he could ever have found in the Jewish traditions.

Even today, there are people who must choose between Christ and family or Christ and their traditional religion.

This blind beggar made the right choice, even though the cost was great.

"The path of the just is as the shining light, that shineth more and more unto the perfect day" (Prov. 4:18).

QUESTIONS FOR PERSONAL REFLECTION
OR GROUP DISCUSSION

1. What are some frequently debated topics in Christian circles?

2. The disciples asked a theological question about the man born blind (v. 2). How would you explain Jesus' reply in your own words?

3. What was Jesus' main concern when He saw the blind man? What does this tell you about His priorities?

4. Which are you more like—the disciples, who wanted to debate the cause of the man's blindness, or Jesus, who wanted to take care of the man's problem? Why?

5. Like the Samaritan woman at the well, the blind man went through several stages of understanding who Jesus was. What were those stages?

6. How was it possible that the religiously trained leaders were so blind to who Jesus was?

7. Restate in your own words Jesus' description of His mission in verse 39. What did He mean?

8. What might be one of your spiritual blind spots? How can you be receptive to Jesus' illumination in this area?

9. How can you act more like Jesus this week in his concern for those who are blind?

Chapter Ten

The Good Shepherd and His Sheep

(John 10)

Perhaps you remember the episode of *Candid Camera* that took place at an exclusive prep school where all of the students were well above average. The *Candid Camera* people posed as career consultants who were going to advise these brilliant young men concerning the careers that would be best suited to them, on the basis of "tests" and "interviews" that seemed (to the students) quite authentic.

One young man eagerly awaited the "counselor's" verdict. Surely the adviser would tell the boy to be a college president or a bank president or perhaps a research scientist. But, no, the "counselor" had other ideas. You should have seen the look on the boy's face when the "counselor" said: "Son, after evaluating your tests and interview, I've decided that the best job for you is—a shepherd."

The student did not know whether to laugh or cry. After all, who in his right mind would want to be a shepherd? Why devote your life to "stupid sheep" that do not seem to have sense enough to find their way home?

John 10 focuses on the image of sheep, sheepfolds, and shepherds. It is a rural and Eastern image, to be sure, but it is an image that can say a great deal to us today, even in our urban, industrialized world. Paul used this image when admonishing the spiritual leaders in the church at Ephesus (Acts 20:28ff.). The truths that cluster around the image of the shepherd and the sheep are found throughout the Bible, and they are important to us today. The symbols that Jesus used help us understand who He is and what He wants to do for us.

Perhaps the easiest way to approach this somewhat complex chapter of John's gospel is to note the three declarations that Jesus made about Himself.

1. "I AM THE DOOR" (10:1–10)

This sermon grew out of our Lord's confrontation with Jewish leaders, following the excommunication of the beggar (John 9). He had briefly spoken to them about light and darkness, but now He changed the image to that of the shepherd and the sheep. Why? Because to the Jewish mind, a "shepherd" was any kind of leader, spiritual or political. People looked on the king and prophets as shepherds. Israel was privileged to be the flock of the Lord (Ps. 100:3). For background, read Isaiah 56:9–12; Jeremiah 23:1–4; 25:32–38; Ezekiel 34; and Zechariah 11.

Jesus opened His sermon with *a familiar illustration* (John 10:1–6), one that every listener would understand. The sheepfold was usually an enclosure made of rocks, with an opening for the door. The shepherd (or a porter) would guard the flock, or flocks, at night by lying across the opening. It was not unusual for several flocks to be sheltered together in the same fold. In the morning, the shepherds would come, call their sheep, and assemble their own flocks. Each sheep recognized its own master's voice.

The true shepherd comes in through the door, and the porter recognizes him. The thieves and robbers could never enter through the door, so they have to climb over the wall and enter the fold through deception. But even if they did get in, they would never get the sheep to follow them, for the sheep follow only the voice of their own shepherd. The false shepherds can never *lead* the sheep, so they must *steal* them away.

It is clear that the listeners did not understand what Jesus said or why He said it. (The word translated "parable" means "a dark saying, a proverb." Our Lord's teaching in John 10 is not like the parables recorded in the other gospels.) The occasion for this lesson was the excommunication of the beggar from the synagogue (John 9:34). The false shepherds did not care for this man; instead, they mistreated him and threw him out. But Jesus, the Shepherd, came to him and took him in (John 9:35–38).

It is unfortunate that John 10:1 is often used to teach that the sheepfold is heaven and that those who try to get in by any way other than Christ are destined to fail. While the teaching is true (Acts 4:12), it is not based on this verse. Jesus made it clear that the fold is the nation of Israel (John 10:16). The Gentiles are the "other sheep" not of the fold of Israel.

When Jesus came to the nation of Israel, He came the appointed way, just as the Scriptures promised. Every true shepherd must be called of God and sent by God. If he truly speaks God's Word, the sheep will "hear his voice" and not be afraid to follow him. The true shepherd will love the sheep and care for them.

Since the people did not understand His symbolic language, Jesus followed the illustration with an *application* (John 10:7–10). Twice He said, "I am the door." He is the Door of the sheepfold and makes it possible for the sheep to *leave* the fold (the religion of Judaism) and to *enter* His flock. The Pharisees *threw* the beggar out of the synagogue, but Jesus *led* him out of Judaism and into the flock of God!

But the Shepherd does not stop with leading the sheep out; He also leads them *in*. They become a part of the "one flock" (not "fold"), which is His church. He is the Door of salvation (John 10:9). Those who trust Him enter into the Lord's flock and fold, and they have the wonderful privilege of going "in and out" and finding pasture. When you keep in mind that the shepherd actually was the "door" of the fold, this image becomes very real.

As the Door, Jesus delivers sinners from bondage and leads them into freedom. They have salvation! This word *saved* means "delivered safe and sound." It was used to say that a person had recovered from severe illness, come through a bad storm, survived a war, or was acquitted at court. Some modern preachers want to do away with an "old-fashioned" word like "saved," but Jesus used it!

Jesus was referring primarily to the religious leaders of that day (John 10:8). He was not condemning every prophet or servant of God who ever ministered before He came to earth. The statement "are thieves and rob-bers" (not "were") makes it clear that He had the present religious leaders in mind. They were not true shepherds, nor did they have the approval of God on their ministry. They did not love the sheep but instead exploited them and abused them. The beggar was a good example of what the "thieves and robbers" could do.

It is clear in the gospel record that the religious rulers of Israel were interested only in providing for themselves and protecting themselves. The Pharisees were covetous (Luke 16:14) and even took advantage of the poor widows (Mark 12:40). They turned God's temple into a den of thieves (Matt. 21:13), and they plotted to kill Jesus so that Rome would not take away their privileges (John 11:49–53).

The True Shepherd came to save the sheep, but the false shepherds take advantage of the sheep and exploit them. Behind these false shepherds is "the thief" (John 10:10), probably a reference to Satan. The thief wants to steal the sheep from the fold, slaughter them, and destroy them. We shall see later that the sheep are safe in the hands of the Shepherd and the Father (John 10:27–29).

When you go through "the Door," you receive life and you are saved. As you go "in and out," you enjoy *abundant* life in the rich pastures of the Lord. His sheep enjoy fullness and freedom. Jesus not only gave His life *for* us, but He gives His life *to* us right now!

The emphasis in this first section is on "the door." Our Lord then shifted the emphasis to "the shepherd" and made a second declaration.

2. "I AM THE GOOD SHEPHERD" (10:11–21)

This is the fourth of our Lord's "I am" statements in John's gospel (John 6:35; 8:12; 10:9). Certainly in making this statement, He is contrasting Himself to the false shepherds who were in charge of the Jewish religion of that day. He had already called them "thieves and robbers," and now He would describe them as "hirelings."

The word translated "good" means "intrinsically good, beautiful, fair." It describes that which is the ideal, the model that others may safely imitate. Our Lord's goodness was inherent in His nature. To call Him "good" is the same as calling Him "God" (Mark 10:17–18).

Some of the greatest people named in the Bible were shepherds by occupation: Abel, the patriarchs, Moses, and David, to name a few. Even today in the Holy Land, you may see shepherds leading flocks and revealing how intimately they know each sheep, its individual traits, and its special needs. Keep in mind that Jewish shepherds did not tend the sheep in order to slaughter them, unless they were used for sacrifice. Shepherds tended them that the sheep might give wool, milk, and lambs.

Jesus pointed out four special ministries that He performs as the Good Shepherd.

(1) He dies for the sheep (vv. 11–13). Under the old dispensation, the sheep died for the shepherd, but now the Good Shepherd dies for the sheep! Five times in this sermon, Jesus clearly affirmed the sacrificial nature of His death (John 10:11, 15, 17–18). He did not die as a martyr, killed by men; He died as a substitute, willingly laying down His life for us.

The fact that Jesus said that He died "for the sheep" must not be isolated from the rest of biblical teaching about the cross. He also died for the nation Israel (John 11:50–52) and for the world (John 6:51). While the blood of Jesus Christ is *sufficient* for the salvation of the world, it is *efficient* only for those who will believe.

Jesus contrasted Himself to the hireling who watches over the sheep only because he is paid to do so. But when there is danger, the hireling runs away, while the true shepherd stays and cares for the flock. The key phrase is "whose own the sheep are not." The Good Shepherd *purchases the sheep,* and they are His because He died for them. They belong to Him, and He cares for them. By nature, sheep are stupid and prone to get into danger, and they need a shepherd to care for them.

Throughout the Bible, God's people are compared to sheep, and the comparison is a good one. Sheep are clean animals, unlike pigs and dogs (2 Peter 2:20–22). They are defenseless and need the care of the shepherd (Ps. 23). They are, to use Wesley's phrase, "prone to wander" and must often be searched for and brought back to the fold (Luke 15:3–7). Sheep are peaceful animals, useful to the shepherd. In these, and other ways, they picture those who have trusted Jesus Christ and are a part of God's flock.

The Pharisees, in contrast to good shepherds, had no loving concern for the beggar, so they put him out of the synagogue. Jesus found him and cared for him.

(2) He knows His sheep (vv. 14–15). In the gospel of John, the word *know* means much more than intellectual awareness. It speaks of an intimate relationship between God and His people (see John 17:3). The Eastern shepherd knows his sheep personally and therefore knows best how to minister to them.

To begin with, our Lord knows our names (see John 10:3). He knew Simon (John 1:42) and even gave him a new name. He called Zacchaeus by name (Luke 19:5), and when He spoke Mary's name in the garden, she recognized her Shepherd (John 20:16). If you have ever had your identity "lost" in a maze of computer operations, then you can appreciate the comforting fact that the Good Shepherd knows each of His sheep by name.

He also knows our natures. While all sheep are alike in their essential nature, each sheep has its own distinctive characteristics, and the loving shepherd recognizes these traits. One sheep may be afraid of high places, another of dark shadows. A faithful shepherd will consider these special needs as he tends the flock.

Have you ever noticed how different the twelve apostles were from one another? Peter was impulsive and outspoken, while Thomas was hesitant and doubting. Andrew was a "people person" who was always bringing somebody to Jesus, while Judas wanted to "use" people in order to get their money for himself. Jesus knew each of the men personally, and He knew exactly how to deal with them.

Because He knows our natures, He also knows our needs. Often, *we* do not even know our own needs! Psalm 23 is a beautiful poetic description of how the Good Shepherd cares for His sheep. In the pastures, by the waters, and even through the valleys, the sheep need not fear, because the shepherd is caring for them and meeting their needs. If you connect Psalm 23:1 and 6, you get the main theme of the poem: "I shall not want … all the days of my life."

As the shepherd cares for the sheep, the sheep get to know their shepherd better. The Good Shepherd knows His sheep, and His sheep know Him. They get to know Him better by listening to His voice (the Word) and experiencing His daily care. As the sheep follow the Shepherd, they learn to love and to trust Him. He loves "his own" (John 13:1), and He shows that love in the way He cares for them.

(3) The Good Shepherd brings other sheep into the flock (v. 16). The "fold" is Judaism (John 10:1), but there is another fold—the Gentiles, who are outside the covenants of Israel (Eph. 2:11ff.). In our Lord's early ministry, He concentrated on the "lost sheep of the house of Israel" (Matt. 10:5–6; 15:24–27). The people converted at Pentecost were Jews and Jewish proselytes (Acts 2:5, 14), but the church was not to remain a "Jewish flock." Peter took the gospel to the Gentiles (Acts 10—11), and Paul carried the message to the Gentiles in the far reaches of the Roman Empire (Acts 13:1ff.).

The phrase "one fold" should read "one flock." There is but one flock, the people of God, who belong to the Good Shepherd. God has His people all over this world (see Acts 18:1–11), and He will call them and gather them together.

The missionary message of the gospel of John is obvious: "For God so loved the world" (John 3:16). Jesus Himself defied custom and witnessed to a Samaritan woman. He refused to defend the exclusivist approach of the Jewish religious leaders. He died for a lost world, and His desire is that His people reach a lost world with the message of eternal life.

(4) The Good Shepherd takes up His life again (vv. 17–21). His voluntary death was followed by His victorious resurrection. From the human point of view, it appeared that Jesus was executed; but from the divine point of view, He laid down His life willingly. When Jesus cried on the cross, "It is finished," He then voluntarily yielded up His spirit to the Father (John 19:30). Three days later, He voluntarily took up His life again and arose from the dead. The Father gave Him this authority in love.

Sometimes the Scriptures teach that it was the Father who raised the Son (Acts 2:32; Rom. 6:4; Heb. 13:20). Here, the Son stated that He had authority to take up His life again. Both are true, for the Father and the Son worked together in perfect harmony (John 5:17, 19). In a previous sermon, Jesus had hinted that He had power to raise Himself from the dead (John 5:26). Of course, this was a claim that the Jews would protest, because it was tantamount to saying "I am God!"

How did the listeners respond to this message? "There was a division therefore again among the Jews" (John 10:19). Note that word *again* (John 7:43; 9:16). The old accusation that Jesus was a demoniac was hurled at Him again (John 7:20; 8:48, 52). People will do almost anything to avoid facing the truth!

Since Jesus Christ is "the Door," we would expect a division, because a door shuts some people in and others out! He is the Good Shepherd, and the Shepherd must separate the sheep from the goats. It is impossible to be neutral about Jesus Christ, for what we believe about Him is a matter of life or death (John 8:24).

His third declaration was the most startling of all.

3. "I Am the Son of God" (10:22–42)

The events in this section occurred about two and a half months after those described in John 10:1–21. John put them together because in both messages Jesus used the imagery of the shepherd and the sheep.

The encounter (vv. 22–24). The Feast of the Dedication (Hanukkah, "the feast of lights") takes place in December, near the time of the Christian Christmas celebration. The feast commemorates the rededication of the temple by Judas Maccabeus in 164 BC, after it had been desecrated by the Seleucids of Syria. This historical fact may bear a relationship to the words of Jesus in John 10:36, for He had been set apart (dedicated) by the Father and sent into the world. The Jewish leaders were celebrating a great event in history yet passing by a great opportunity right in their own temple!

The leaders surrounded Jesus in the temple so that He had to stop and listen to them. They had decided that it was time for a "showdown," and they did not want Him to evade the issue any longer. "How long are You going to hold us in suspense?" they kept saying to Him. "Tell us plainly— are You the Messiah?"

The explanation (vv. 25–42). Jesus reminded them of what He had already taught them. He emphasized the witness of His *words* ("I told you") and His *works* (see John 5:17ff. and 7:14ff. for similar replies).

But our Lord went much deeper in His explanation this time, for He revealed to the Jewish leaders *why* they did not understand His words or grasp the significance of His works: They were not His sheep. From the human standpoint, we become His sheep by believing, but from the divine standpoint, we believe because we are His sheep. There is a mystery here that we cannot fathom or explain, but we can accept it and rejoice (Rom. 11:33–36). God has His sheep, and He knows who they are. They will hear His voice and respond.

The lost sinner who hears God's Word knows nothing about divine election. He hears only that Christ died for the sins of the world and that he may receive the gift of eternal life by trusting the Savior. When he trusts the Savior, he becomes a member of God's family and a sheep in the flock. Then he learns that he was "chosen … in him [Christ] before the foundation of the world" (Eph. 1:4). He also learns that each saved sinner is the Father's "love gift" to His Son (see John 10:29; 17:2, 6, 9, 11–12, 24).

In the Bible, divine election and human responsibility are perfectly balanced, and what God has joined together, we must not put asunder.

Jesus went on to explain that His sheep are secure in His hand and in the Father's hand. "They shall never perish" is His promise (John 3:16; 6:39; 17:12; 18:9). The false shepherds bring destruction (John 10:10, same Greek word), but the Good Shepherd sees to it that His sheep shall never perish.

The security of God's sheep is assured here in several ways. First, by definition—we have "eternal life," and that cannot be conditional and still be eternal. Second, this life is a gift, not something that we earn or merit. If we were not saved by our own good works, but by His grace, then we cannot be lost by our bad works (Rom. 11:6). But most important, Jesus gave us His promise that His sheep do not perish and that His promise cannot be broken.

It is important to keep in mind that Jesus was talking about sheep—true believers—and not counterfeits. The dog and the pig will go back into sin (2 Peter 2:20–22), but the sheep, being a clean animal, will follow the Shepherd into the green pastures. The false professor will talk about his faith and even his works, but he will never make it into heaven (Matt. 7:13–29). Most of us know people who professed to be saved and then went back into sin, but their doing so only proved that they never really trusted Christ to begin with. Jesus did not promise security to anyone but His true sheep.

As you review our Lord's teaching about His ministry as the Good Shepherd, you note that He has a threefold relationship to His sheep. He has a *loving* relationship because He died for the sheep, as well as a *living* relationship because He cares for the sheep. It is also a *lasting* relationship, for He keeps His sheep and not a one is lost.

Our Lord made a statement that He knew would startle His enemies and give them more reason to oppose Him (John 10:30). It was the "plain answer" that the religious leaders had asked for. "I and my Father are one" is as clear a statement of His deity as you will find anywhere in Scripture. This was even stronger than His statement that He had come down from heaven (John 6) or that He existed before Abraham ever lived (John 8:58).

The word *one* does not suggest that the Father and the Son are identical persons. Rather, it means that they are one in essence: The Father is God and the Son is God, but the Father is not the Son, and the Son is not the Father. He is speaking about unity, not identity. (See John 17:21–24 for similar language.)

The Jewish leaders understood clearly what He was saying! Some modern liberal theologians would water down our Lord's statement, but the people who heard it knew exactly what He was saying: "I am God!" (Note John 10:33.) To speak this way, of course, was blasphemy, and according to Jewish belief, blasphemy had to be punished by being put to death (see Lev. 24:16; Num. 15:30ff.; Deut. 21:22).

Our Lord used Psalm 82:6 to refute their accusation and halt their actions. The picture in Psalm 82 is that of a court, where God has assembled the judges of the earth, to warn them that they too will one day be judged. The Hebrew word *elohim* can be translated as "god" or as "judges," as in Exodus 21:6 and 22:8–9. It is also one of the Old Testament names for God. The Jewish rulers certainly knew their own language, and they knew that Jesus was speaking the truth. If God called human judges "gods," then why should they stone Him for applying the same title to Himself?

John 10:36 is crucial because it gives a double affirmation of the deity of Christ. First, the Father sanctified (set apart) the Son and sent Him into the world; and second, Jesus stated boldly, "I am the Son of God" (see John 5:25). He gave them the "plain answer" they asked for, but they would not believe it!

Could they have believed? Jesus *invited* them, urged them, to believe, if only on the basis of His miracles (John 10:37–38). If they would believe the miracles, then they would know the Father, and that would open the way for them to know the Son and believe in Him. It was simply a matter of examining the evidence honestly and being willing to accept the truth.

Once again, they tried to arrest Him (see John 7:44; 8:59), but He escaped and left the area completely. He did not return to Jerusalem until "Palm Sunday," when He presented Himself as Israel's King.

John the Baptist had ministered at Bethabara (John 1:28), but we are not sure where this was. It was on the other side of the Jordan River, perhaps eighteen to twenty miles from Jerusalem. Some maps put it almost directly across from Jerusalem, just east of Jericho.

Why did Jesus go there? For one thing, it was a safe retreat; the Jewish religious leaders were not likely to follow Him there. Also, it was a good place to prepare for His final week of public ministry when He would lay down His life for the sheep. As He remembered His own baptism by John and all that He had experienced at that time (Matt. 3:13–17; John 1:20–34), it must have fortified Him for the suffering that He knew He must endure.

The common people continued to seek Jesus, and He continued to minister to them. It is worth noting that John the Baptist's witness was still bearing fruit long after he was dead! His witness to Jesus Christ led many to trust the Savior. John was not a miracle worker, but he was a faithful witness who pointed to Jesus Christ. "He must increase, but I must decrease" (John 3:30).

Have you responded personally to our Lord's three great declarations recorded in this chapter?

He is the Door. Have you "entered in" by faith so that you are saved?

He is the Good Shepherd. Have you heard His voice and trusted Him? After all, He laid down His life for you!

He is the Son of God. Do you believe that? Have you given yourself to Him and received eternal life?

Remember His stern warning: "If ye believe not that I am he, ye shall die in your sins" (John 8:24).

QUESTIONS FOR PERSONAL REFLECTION
OR GROUP DISCUSSION

1. Who are some people you have "followed" in the past?

2. Read verses 1–10. How is Jesus like a door into the sheepfold?

3. How have you experienced Him as a door like this?

4. Who would Jesus call thieves today? Why?

5. Read verses 11–21. What did Jesus mean when He said, "I am the good shepherd"? How is He like a shepherd?

6. How was Jesus different from the religious leaders of His day?

7. Has Jesus been a Good Shepherd to you? If so, how? If you have complaints, what are they?

8. Although Jesus' audience knew much about shepherds, people in our culture generally don't. To whom do you think Jesus would compare Himself today? Why? *Ship's Captain*
? Billy Graham

9. Read verses 22–42. Why do you think the people so violently rejected Jesus' teaching that "I and the Father are one"? Why didn't they believe Him?

10. How can you follow your Shepherd more closely this week?

Chapter Eleven

THE LAST MIRACLE, THE LAST ENEMY

(John 11)

The raising of Lazarus from the dead was not our Lord's last miracle before the cross, but it was certainly His greatest and the one that aroused the most response from both His friends and His enemies. John selected this miracle as the seventh in the series recorded in his book because it was really the climactic miracle of our Lord's earthly ministry. He had raised others from the dead, but Lazarus had been in the grave four days. It was a miracle that could not be denied or avoided by the Jewish leaders.

If Jesus Christ can do nothing about death, then whatever else He can do amounts to nothing. "If in this life only we have hope in Christ, we are of all men most miserable" (1 Cor. 15:19). Death is man's last enemy (1 Cor. 15:26), but Jesus Christ has defeated this horrible enemy totally and permanently.

The emphasis in John 11 is on faith; you find some form of the word *believe* at least eight times in this account. Another theme is "the glory of God" (John 11:4, 40). In what Jesus said and did, He sought to strengthen the faith of three groups of people.

1. THE DISCIPLES (11:1–16)

We sometimes think of the disciples as "supersaints," but such was not the case. They often failed their Lord, and He was constantly seeking to increase their faith. After all, one day He would leave them, and they would have the responsibility of carrying on the ministry. If their faith was weak, their work could never be strong.

Jesus was at Bethabara, about twenty miles from Bethany (John 1:28; 10:40). One day, a messenger arrived with the sad news that our Lord's dear friend Lazarus was sick. If the man had traveled quickly, without any delay, he could have made the trip in one day. Jesus sent him back the next day with the encouraging message recorded in John 11:4. Then Jesus waited two more days before He left for Bethany, and by the time He and His disciples arrived, Lazarus had been dead for four days. This means that Lazarus had died *the very day* the messenger left to contact Jesus!

The schedule of events would look something like this, allowing one day for travel:

Day 1—The messenger comes to Jesus (Lazarus dies).

Day 2—The messenger returns to Bethany.

Day 3—Jesus waits another day, then departs.

Day 4—Jesus arrives in Bethany.

When the messenger arrived back home, he would find Lazarus already dead. What would his message convey to the grieving sisters now that their brother was already dead and buried? Jesus was urging them to believe His word no matter how discouraging the circumstances might appear.

No doubt the disciples were perplexed about several matters. First of all, if Jesus loved Lazarus so much, why did He permit him to get sick? Even more, why did He delay to go to the sisters? For that matter, could

He not have healed Lazarus at a distance, as He did the nobleman's son (John 4:43–54)? The record makes it clear that there was a strong love relationship between Jesus and this family (John 11:3, 5, 36), and yet our Lord's behavior seems to contradict this love.

God's love for His own is not a pampering love; it is a perfecting love. The fact that He loves us and we love Him is no guarantee that we will be sheltered from the problems and pains of life. After all, the Father loves His Son, and yet the Father permitted His beloved Son to drink the cup of sorrow and experience the shame and pain of the cross. We must never think that love and suffering are incompatible. Certainly they unite in Jesus Christ.

Jesus could have prevented Lazarus's sickness or even healed it from where He was, but He chose not to. He saw in this sickness an opportunity to glorify the Father. It is not important that we Christians are comfortable, but it is important that we glorify God in all that we do.

In their "prayer" to Jesus, the two sisters did not tell Him what to do. They simply informed Him that there was a need, and they reminded Him of His love for Lazarus. They knew that it was dangerous for Jesus to return to Judea because the Jewish leaders were out to destroy Him. Perhaps they hoped that He would "speak the word" and that their brother would be restored to health.

Our Lord's message to the sisters did not say that their brother would not die. It promised only that death would not be the *ultimate* result, for the ultimate result would be the glory of God. (Note that once again, Jesus called Himself "the Son of God.") He wanted them to lay hold of this promise; in fact, He reminded Martha of this message when she balked at having the tomb opened (John 11:40).

When we find ourselves confronted by disease, disappointment, delay, and even death, our only encouragement is the Word of God. We must live by faith and not by sight. Their situation seemed hopeless, yet the sisters knew that Jesus was the Master of every situation. The promise in Psalm 50:15 finds a parallel here: "And call upon me in the day of trouble: I will deliver thee, and thou shalt glorify me."

What about our Lord's delay? He was not waiting for Lazarus to die, for he was already dead. Jesus lived on a divine timetable (John 11:9), and He was waiting for the Father to tell Him when to go to Bethany. The fact that the man had been dead four days gave greater authenticity to the miracle and greater opportunity for people to believe, including His own disciples (see John 11:15).

When our Lord announced that He was returning to Judea, His disciples were alarmed, because they knew how dangerous it would be. (Bethany is only about two miles from Jerusalem.) But Jesus was willing to lay down His life for His friends (John 15:13). He knew that His return to Judea and the miracle of raising Lazarus would precipitate His own arrest and death.

The Lord calmed their fears by reminding them that He was on the Father's schedule and that nothing could harm them. As we have seen, this is an important theme in the gospel of John (John 2:4; 7:6, 8, 30; 8:20; 12:23; 13:1; 17:1). But the disciples not only misunderstood the schedule, they also misunderstood the reason for the visit. They thought that, if Lazarus was sleeping, he was getting better! It was another example of their inability to grasp spiritual truth. "If he is sleeping, he must be improving—so let's not bother to go to Bethany!"

Then He told them openly that Lazarus was dead. (Death for the believer is compared to sleep. See Acts 7:60; 1 Cor. 15:51; 1 Thess. 4:13–18.) He did not say He was glad that His friend died, but that He was glad He had not been there, for now He could reveal to His disciples His mighty power. The result would be glory to God and the strengthening of their faith.

If Thomas's attitude was any indication, the faith of the disciples certainly needed strengthening! The name Thomas means "twin" in the

Aramaic language; the Greek equivalent is Didymus. We do not know whose twin he was, but there are times when *all of us* seem to be his twin when we consider our unbelief and depressed feelings! It was Thomas who demanded evidence before he would accept the truth of our Lord's resurrection (John 20:24–28).

Thomas was a doubting man, but we must confess that he was a devoted man: He was willing to go with Jesus into danger and risk his own life. We may not admire his faith, but we can certainly applaud his loyalty and courage.

2. The Sisters (11:17–40)

Jesus was concerned not only about the faith of His own disciples, but also about the faith of Mary and Martha (John 11:26, 40). Each experience of suffering and trial ought to increase our faith, but this kind of spiritual growth is not automatic. We must respond positively to the ministry of the Word and the Spirit of God. Jesus had sent a promise to the two sisters (John 11:4), and now He would discover how they had received it.

The event recorded in Luke 10:38–42 makes it clear that Mary and Martha were quite different in their personalities. Martha was the worker, the active one, while Mary was the contemplative one who sat at the feet of Jesus and listened to His words. Jesus did not condemn Martha's service, but He did rebuke her for being "torn apart" by so many things. She needed to have priorities and center her activities on the things that God would approve. As an old Wesley hymn puts it, we need to have a balanced life:

> Faithful to my Lord's commands,
> I still would choose the better part:
> Serve with careful Martha's hands
> And loving Mary's heart.

We would expect Martha to rush out to meet Jesus while Mary sat in the house, weeping with her friends. Since Mary later echoed Martha's words of greeting (John 11:32), it is likely that the sisters often said these words to each other as they waited for Jesus to arrive. While there may have been a tinge of disappointment in the statement, there was also evidence of faith, for nobody ever died in the presence of Jesus Christ. "If" is such a big word! How futile it is to imagine what might have been, if—!

Martha was quick to affirm her faith in Jesus Christ (John 11:22), and Jesus responded to that faith by promising her that her brother would rise again. He was thinking of the immediate situation, but she interpreted His words to mean the future resurrection in the last day (Dan. 12:2–3; John 5:28–29). Here is another instance in John's gospel of people lacking spiritual perception and being unable to understand the words of Jesus.

Our Lord's reply is the fifth of the "I am" statements. It is important to note that Jesus did not deny what Martha said about the future resurrection. The resurrection of the human body is a cardinal doctrine in the orthodox Jewish faith. But in His great "I am" statement, our Lord completely transformed the doctrine of the resurrection and, in so doing, brought great comfort to Martha's heart.

To begin with, He brought the doctrine of the resurrection out of the shadows and into the light. The Old Testament revelation about death and resurrection is not clear or complete; it is, as it were, "in the shadows." In fact, there are some passages in Psalms and Ecclesiastes that almost make one believe that death is the end and there is no hope beyond the grave. False teachers like to use these passages to support their heretical teachings, but they ignore (or misinterpret) the clear teachings found in the New Testament. After all, it was not David or Solomon who "brought life and immortality to light through the gospel" (2 Tim. 1:10), but Jesus Christ!

By His teaching, His miracles, and His own resurrection, Jesus clearly taught the resurrection of the human body. He has declared once for all that death is real, that there is life after death, and that the body will one day be raised by the power of God.

He transformed this doctrine in a second way: He took it out of a book and put it into a person, Himself. "I am the resurrection and the life" (John 11:25)! While we thank God for what the Bible teaches (and all Martha had was the Old Testament), we realize that we are saved by the Redeemer, Jesus Christ, and not by a doctrine written in a book. When we know Him by faith, we need not fear the shadow of death.

When you are sick, you want a doctor and not a medical book or a formula. When you are being sued, you want a lawyer and not a law book. Likewise, when you face your last enemy, death, you want the Savior and not a doctrine written in a book. In Jesus Christ, every doctrine is made personal (1 Cor. 1:30). When you belong to Him, you have all that you ever will need in life, death, time, or eternity!

But perhaps the greatest transformation Jesus performed was to move the doctrine of the resurrection out of the future and into the present. Martha was looking to the future, knowing that Lazarus would rise again and that she would see him. Her friends were looking to the past and saying, "He could have prevented Lazarus from dying" (John 11:37)! But Jesus tried to center their attention on the *present:* Wherever He is, God's resurrection power is available *now* (Rom. 6:4; Gal. 2:20; Phil. 3:10).

Jesus affirmed that believers would one day be raised from the dead (John 11:25). Then He immediately revealed the added truth that some believers would never die (and it is a double negative, "never never die!") (John 11:26). How is this possible? The answer is found in 1 Thessalonians 4:13–18. When Jesus Christ returns in the air to take His people home, those who are alive at His coming shall never die. They shall be changed and caught up to meet Him in the air!

Martha did not hesitate to affirm her faith. She used three different titles for Jesus: Lord, Christ (Messiah), and Son of God. The words "I believe" are in the perfect tense, indicating a fixed and settled faith. "I have believed and I will continue to believe!"

Our Lord dealt with Martha's faith; now He had to help Mary. Why did Martha call Mary "secretly"? Possibly because of the danger involved: They knew that the Jewish leaders were out to arrest Jesus. When Mary arose to go to meet Jesus, her friends misunderstood her actions and thought she was going to the tomb to weep. They wanted to weep with her, so they followed along. Imagine their surprise when they met Jesus!

Mary is found three times in the gospel record, and each time she is at the feet of Jesus (Luke 10:39; John 11:32; 12:3). She sat at His feet and listened to His word, she fell at His feet and poured out her sorrow, and she came to His feet to give Him her praise and worship. Mary's only recorded words in the Gospels are given in John 11:32, and they echo what Martha had already said (John 11:21).

Mary did not say much because she was overcome with sorrow and began to weep. Her friends joined in the weeping, as Jewish people are accustomed to do. The word used means "a loud weeping, a lamentation." Our Lord's response was to groan within and "be moved with indignation." At what was He indignant? At the ravages of sin in the world that He had created. Death is an enemy, and Satan uses the fear of death as a terrible weapon (Heb. 2:14–18). No wonder Jesus was indignant!

The mystery of our Lord's incarnation is seen by His question in John 11:34. Jesus knew that Lazarus had died (John 11:11), but He had to ask where he was buried. Our Lord never used His divine powers when normal human means would suffice.

"Jesus wept" is the shortest and yet the deepest verse in Scripture. His was a silent weeping (the Greek word is used nowhere else in the New

Testament) and not the loud lamentation of the mourners. But why did He weep at all? After all, He knew that He would raise Lazarus from the dead (John 11:11).

Our Lord's weeping reveals the humanity of the Savior. He has entered into all of our experiences and knows how we feel. In fact, being the perfect God-man, Jesus experienced these things in a deeper way than we do. His tears also assure us of His sympathy; He is indeed "a man of sorrows and acquainted with grief" (Isa. 53:3). Today, He is our merciful and faithful High Priest, and we may come to the throne of grace and find all the gracious help that we need (Heb. 4:14–16).

We see in His tears the tragedy of sin but also the glory of heaven. Perhaps Jesus was weeping *for* Lazarus, as well as *with* the sisters, because He knew He was calling His friend from heaven and back into a wicked world where he would one day have to die again. Jesus had come down from heaven; He knew what Lazarus was leaving behind.

The spectators saw in His tears an evidence of His love. But some of them said, "If Jesus loved Lazarus so much, why did He not prevent his death?" Perhaps they were thinking, "Jesus is weeping because He was unable to do anything. They are tears of deep regret." In other words, *nobody present really expected a miracle!* For this reason, nobody could accuse Jesus of "plotting" this event and being in collusion with the two sisters and their friends. Even the disciples did not believe that Jesus would raise Lazarus from the dead!

The one person who declared her faith was Martha (John 11:27), and she failed at the last minute. "Open the tomb? By now he smells!" Jesus gently reminded her of the message He had sent at least three days before (John 11:4), and He urged her to believe it. True faith relies on God's promises and thereby releases God's power. Martha relented, and the stone was rolled away.

3. THE JEWS (11:41–57)

The emphasis from this point on was on the faith of the spectators, the people who had come to comfort Mary and Martha. Jesus paused to pray (John 11:41; see also 6:11) and thanked the Father that the prayer had already been heard. When had He prayed? Probably when He received the message that His friend was sick (John 11:4). The Father then told Him what the plan was, and Jesus obeyed the Father's will. His prayer now was for the sake of the unbelieving spectators, that they might know that God had sent Him.

A quaint Puritan writer said that if Jesus had not named Lazarus when He shouted, He would have emptied the whole cemetery! Jesus called *Lazarus* and raised him from the dead. Since Lazarus was bound, he could not walk to the door of the tomb, so God's power must have carried him along. It was an unquestioned miracle that even the most hostile spectator could not deny.

The experience of Lazarus is a good illustration of what happens to a sinner when he trusts the Savior (Eph. 2:1–10). Lazarus was dead, and all sinners are dead. He was decayed, because death and decay go together. All lost people are spiritually dead, but some are more "decayed" than others. No one can be "more dead" than another.

Lazarus was raised from the dead by the power of God, and all who trust Christ have been given new life and lifted out of the graveyard of sin (see John 5:24). Lazarus was set free from the graveclothes (see Col. 3:1ff.) and given new liberty. You find him seated with Christ at the table (John 12:2), and all believers are "seated with Christ" in heavenly places (Eph. 2:6), enjoying spiritual food and fellowship.

Because of the great change in Lazarus, many people desired to see him, and his "living witness" was used by God to bring people to salvation (John 12:9–11). There are no recorded words of Lazarus in the Gospels, but his daily walk is enough to convince people that Jesus is the Son of God. Because of his effective witness, Lazarus was persecuted by the religious leaders who wanted to kill him and get rid of the evidence.

As with the previous miracles, the people were divided in their response. Some did believe and on "Palm Sunday" gave witness of the miracle Jesus had performed (John 12:17–18). But others immediately went to the religious leaders and reported what had happened in Bethany. These "informers" were so near the kingdom, yet there is no evidence that they believed. If the heart will not yield to truth, then the grace of God cannot bring salvation. These people could have experienced a spiritual resurrection in their own lives!

It was necessary that the Jewish council (Sanhedrin) meet and discuss what to do with Jesus. They were not seeking after truth; they were seeking for ways to protect their own selfish interests. If He gathered too many followers, He might get the attention of the Roman authorities, and this could hurt the Jewish cause.

The high priest, Caiaphas, was a Sadducee, not a Pharisee (Acts 23:6–10); but the two factions could always get together to fight a common enemy. Unknown to himself and to the council, Caiaphas uttered a divine prophecy: Jesus would die for the nation so that the nation would not perish. "For the transgression of my people was he stricken" (Isa. 53:8). True to his vision of a worldwide family of God, John added his inspired explanation: Jesus would die not only for the Jews, but for all of God's children who would be gathered together in one heavenly family. (Note John 4:42; 10:16.)

The official decision that day was that Jesus must die (see Matt. 12:14; Luke 19:47; John 5:18; 7:1, 19–20, 25). The leaders thought that *they* were in control of the situation, but it was God who was working out His predetermined plan (Acts 2:23). Originally, they wanted to wait until after the Passover, but God had decreed otherwise.

Jesus withdrew to Ephraim, about fifteen miles north of Jerusalem, and there He remained in quiet retirement with His disciples. The crowd was gathering in Jerusalem for the Passover Feast, and the pilgrims were wondering if Jesus would attend the feast even though He was in danger. He was now on the "wanted" list, because the council had made it known that anyone who knew where Jesus was must report it to the officials.

John 11 reveals the deity of Jesus Christ and the utter depravity of the human heart. The rich man in hades had argued, "If one went unto them from the dead, they will repent" (Luke 16:30). Lazarus came back from the dead, and the officials wanted to kill him! Miracles certainly reveal the power of God, but of themselves they cannot communicate the grace of God.

The stage had been set for the greatest drama in history, during which humanity would do its worst and God would give His best.

> O come, let us adore Him,
> Christ, the Lord!

QUESTIONS FOR PERSONAL REFLECTION
OR GROUP DISCUSSION

1. How have you reacted when someone you loved died?

   Sadness - wishing it hadn't happened. Older friends/family expected - end of a full life - wishing for more time. Christians knowing we'll meet again. Unexpected tragedies - harder to understand.

2. Read verses 1–16. Why was it dangerous for Jesus to go to Bethany at that time? *The leaders had already tried to seize Him & stone Him. Close to Jerusalem, where leaders were.*

3. Why did Jesus wait to go see Lazarus? What do you learn about Him from His decision to wait? *He was tuned to His Father's timetable & direction.*

4. Read verses 17–40. What beliefs and emotions do you sense in Martha's and Mary's reactions to Jesus? *Beliefs that Jesus is God's Son & they will trust Him whatever life gives them.*

5. What did Jesus mean when He said, "I am the resurrection and the life"? *Jesus is the resurrected one - He is the one who triumphed over death, and released His believers from death's grip.*

6. How is resurrection different from reincarnation?

   Resurrection - transformed body - same spirit alive.

7. How does the resurrection of the human body, as opposed to just the immortality of souls floating in heaven, matter to us? How should our hope of resurrection affect our lives now? Our view of bodies?

8. What does Jesus' response to Lazarus's death reveal about Him?

9. Read verses 41–57. Why did the religious leaders meet to decide what to do about Jesus?

10. In what ways did John emphasize faith in this chapter?

11. How can you exercise faith in Jesus when something tragic happens, like the death of a friend or family member?

Chapter Twelve

CHRIST AND THE CRISIS

(John 12)

John 12 records the second major crisis in the ministry of our Lord as seen by John the apostle. The first occurred when many of His disciples would no longer walk with Him (John 6:66), even though He is "the way" (John 14:6). In this chapter, John tells us that many would not believe in Him (John 12:37ff.), even though He is "the truth." The third crisis will come in John 19: Even though He is "the life," the leaders crucified Him.

John opened his book by telling us that Jesus "came unto his own [world], and his own [people] received him not" (John 1:11). In the first twelve chapters, John presented one witness after another, and one proof after another, to convince us that Jesus is indeed the Christ, the Son of God. All of this evidence was seen firsthand by the leaders of the nation, and yet they rejected His claims. Having been rejected by His own nation, Jesus then retired with His own disciples (John 13:1), whom he loved to the uttermost.

We see in John 12 the Lord Jesus Christ as He relates to four different groups of people, and there are lessons that we can learn as we study this section.

1. Jesus and His Friends (John 12:1–11)

Our Lord knew that the Jewish leaders were out to arrest Him and kill Him (John 11:53, 57), but He still returned to Bethany, only two miles from the very citadel of His enemies. Why? So that He might spend a quiet time with His dear friends Mary, Martha, and Lazarus. True to their personalities, Martha busily served, and Mary worshipped at the feet of Jesus (see Luke 10:38–42).

The account of Mary's anointing of her Lord is found also in Matthew 26:6–13 and Mark 14:3–9. But it must not be confused with the account given in Luke 7:36–50, where a former harlot anointed Jesus in the house of Simon the Pharisee. Mary was a virtuous woman, and she anointed Jesus in the house of Simon the (former) leper (Mark 14:3). The Luke 7 event took place in Galilee, while the account we are now considering occurred in Judea. The fact that there are two "Simons" involved should not surprise us, for Simon was a common name in that day.

When you combine all three accounts, you learn that Mary anointed both His head and His feet. It was an act of pure love on her part, for she knew her Lord was about to endure suffering and death. Because she sat at Jesus' feet and listened to Him speak, she knew what He was going to do. It is significant that Mary of Bethany was not one of the women who went to the tomb to anoint the body of Jesus (Mark 16:1).

In a sense, Mary was showing her devotion to Jesus *before* it was too late. She was "giving the roses" while He was yet alive, and not bringing them to the funeral! Her act of love and worship was public, spontaneous, sacrificial, lavish, personal, and unembarrassed. Jesus called it "a good work" (Matt. 26:10; Mark 14:6) and both commended her and defended her.

It would have required a year's wages from a common laborer to purchase that ointment. Like David, Mary would not give to the Lord that which cost her nothing (2 Sam. 24:24). Her beautiful act of worship brought a fragrance to the very house in which they were dining, and the blessing of her deed has spread around the world (Matt. 26:13; Mark 14:9). Little did Mary realize that night that her love for Christ would be a blessing to believers around the world for centuries to come!

When she came to the feet of Jesus, Mary took the place of a slave. When she undid her hair (something Jewish women did not do in public), she humbled herself and laid her glory at His feet (see 1 Cor. 11:15). Of course, she was misunderstood and criticized, but that is what usually happens when somebody gives his or her best to the Lord.

It was Judas who started the criticism, and, sad to say, the other disciples took it up. They did not know that Judas was a devil (John 6:70), and they admired him for his concern for the poor. After all, he was the treasurer, and especially at Passover season, he would want to share with those who were less fortunate (see John 13:21–30). Until the very end, the disciples believed that Judas was a devoted follower of the Lord.

John 12:4–6 records Judas's first words found anywhere in the four gospels. His last words are found in Matthew 27:4. Judas was a thief and was in the habit of stealing money from the money box that he carried. (The Greek word translated "bag" meant originally a small case in which mouthpieces were kept for wind instruments. Then it came to mean any small box and especially a money box. The Greek version of the Old Testament uses this word in 2 Chronicles 24:8–10 for King Joash's money chest.) No doubt Judas had already decided to abandon Jesus, and he wanted to get what he could out of what he considered a bad situation. Perhaps he had hoped that Jesus would defeat Rome and set up the kingdom; in which case, Judas would have been treasurer of the kingdom!

What Mary did was a blessing to Jesus and a blessing to her own life. She was also a blessing to the home, filling it with fragrance (see Phil. 4:18), and today, she is a blessing to the church around the world. Her one act of devotion in the little village of Bethany still sends "ripples of blessing."

But not so Judas! We call our daughters "Mary," but no parent would call a son "Judas." His very name is listed in the dictionary as a synonym for treachery. Mary and Judas are seen in contrast in Proverbs 10:7—"The memory of the just is blessed: but the name of the wicked shall rot." "A good name is better than precious ointment," says Ecclesiastes 7:1, and Mary had both.

Matthew 26:14 gives the impression that immediately after this rebuke, Judas went to the priests and bargained to deliver Jesus into their hands. But it is likely that the events recorded in Matthew 21—25 took place first. No doubt the Lord's rebuke of Judas at Bethany played an important part in his decision actually to betray Jesus. Also, the fact that Jesus once again openly announced His death would motivate Judas to escape while the opportunity was there.

As we look at this event, we see some "representative people" who are examples to us. Martha represents *work* as she served the dinner she had prepared for the Lord. This was just as much a "fragrant offering" as was Mary's ointment (see Heb. 13:16). Mary represents *worship,* and Lazarus represents *witness* (John 11:9–11). People went to Bethany just to be able to see this man who had been raised from the dead!

As mentioned we have no recorded words from Lazarus in the New Testament, but his miraculous life was an effective witness for Jesus Christ. (In contrast, John the Baptist did no miracles, yet his words brought people to Jesus. See John 10:40–42.) We today ought to "walk in newness of life" (Rom. 6:4) because we have been raised from the dead (Eph. 2:1–10; Col. 3:1ff.). Actually, the Christian life ought to be a beautiful balance of worship, work, and witness.

But the fact that Lazarus was a walking miracle put him into a place of danger: The Jewish leaders wanted to kill *him* as well as Jesus! Our Lord was right when He called them children of the Devil, for they were murderers indeed (John 8:42–44). They threw the healed blind man out of the synagogue rather than permit him to bear witness to Christ every Sabbath, and they tried to put Lazarus back into the tomb because he was leading people to faith in Christ. If you will not accept the evidence, you must try to get rid of it!

This quiet evening of fellowship—in spite of the cruel way the disciples treated Mary—must have brought special encouragement and strength to the Savior's heart as He faced the demands of that last week before the cross. We should examine our own hearts and homes to ask whether we are bringing joy to His heart by our worship, work, and witness.

2. JESUS AND THE PASSOVER PILGRIMS (12:12–19)

John shifted the scene from a quiet dinner in Bethany to a noisy public parade in Jerusalem. All four gospels record this event, and their accounts should be compared. This was the only "public demonstration" that our Lord allowed while He was ministering on earth. His purpose was to fulfill the Old Testament prophecy (Zech. 9:9). The result was a growing animosity on the part of the religious leaders, leading eventually to the crucifixion of the Savior.

There were three different groups in the crowd that day: (1) the Passover visitors from outside Judea (John 12:12, 18); (2) the local people who had witnessed the raising of Lazarus (John 12:17); and (3) the religious leaders who were greatly concerned about what Jesus might do at the feast (John 12:19). At each of the different feasts, the people were in keen expectation, wondering if Jesus would be there and what He would do. It looked as though Jesus was actually seeking to incite a revolution and establish Himself as King, but that was not what He had in mind.

What did this event mean to Jesus? For one thing, it was a part of His obedience to the Father's will. The prophet Zechariah (Zech. 9:9) prophesied that the Messiah would enter Jerusalem in that manner, and He fulfilled the prophecy. "Daughter of Zion" is another name for the city of Jerusalem (Jer. 4:31; Lam. 2:4, 8, 10). Certainly Jesus was openly announcing to the people that He indeed is the King of Israel (John 1:49), the promised Messiah. No doubt many of the pilgrims hoped that *now* He would defeat the Romans and set the nation of Israel free.

What did this demonstration mean to the Romans? Nothing is recorded about the Roman viewpoint, but it is certain that they kept a close watch that day. During the annual Passover Feast, it was not uncommon for some of the Jewish nationalists to try to arouse the people, and perhaps they thought this parade was that kind of an event. I imagine that some of the Roman soldiers must have smiled at the "triumphal entry," because it was nothing like their own "Roman triumph" celebrations in the city of Rome.

Whenever a Roman general was victorious on foreign soil, killing at least five thousand of the enemy and gaining new territory, he was given a "Roman triumph" when he returned to the city. It was the Roman equivalent of the American "ticker-tape parade," only with much more splendor. The victor would be permitted to display the trophies he had won and the enemy leaders he had captured. The parade ended at the arena, where some of the captives entertained the people by fighting wild beasts. Compared to a "Roman triumph," our Lord's entry into Jerusalem was nothing.

What did the "triumphal entry" mean to the people of Israel? The pilgrims welcomed Jesus, spread their garments before Him, and waved palm branches as symbols of peace and victory (Rev. 7:9). They quoted from Psalm 118:26, which is a messianic psalm, and they proclaimed Him the "King of Israel." But while they were doing this, Jesus was weeping (Luke 19:37–44)!

The name *Jerusalem* means "city of peace" or "foundation of peace," and the people were hoping that Jesus would bring them the peace that they needed. However, He wept because He saw what lay ahead of the nation—war, suffering, destruction, and a scattered people. At His birth, the angels announced "peace on earth" (Luke 2:13–14), but in His ministry Jesus announced "war on earth" (Luke 12:51ff.). It is significant that the crowds shouted "peace in heaven" (Luke 19:38), because that is the only place where there is peace today!

The nation had wasted its opportunities; its leaders did not know the time of God's visitation. They were ignorant of their own Scriptures. The next time Israel sees the King, the scene will be radically different (Rev. 19:11ff.)! He will come in glory, not in humility, and the armies of heaven will accompany Him. It will be a scene of victory as He comes to defeat His enemies and establish His kingdom.

It is a repeated theme in Scripture that there can be no glory unless first there is suffering. Jesus knew that He must die on the cross before He could enter into His glory (Luke 24:26). The Jewish theologians were not clear in their minds concerning the sufferings of the Messiah and the glorious kingdom that the prophets announced. Some teachers held that there were two Messiahs, one who would suffer and one who would reign. Even our Lord's own disciples were not clear as to what was going on (see John 11:16).

How did the Jewish leaders respond to the "triumphal entry" of the Lord? As they watched the great crowd gather and honor Jesus, the Pharisees were quite sure that Jesus had won the day. They were anticipating some kind of general revolt during the Passover season. Perhaps Jesus would perform a great miracle and in that way capture the minds and hearts of the restless people. How little they really understood the mind and heart of the Master! What they did not realize was that Jesus was "forcing their hand" so that the Sanhedrin would act *during the feast.* The Lamb of God had to give His life when the Passover lambs were being slain.

The statement, "Behold, the world is gone after him!" (John 12:19) was both an exaggeration and a prophecy. In the next section, we meet some visitors from outside Israel.

3. JESUS AND THE GENTILE VISITORS (12:20–36)

Following His entry into Jerusalem, our Lord cleansed the temple for the second time. He quoted Isaiah 56:7 and Jeremiah 7:11: "Is it not written, My house shall be called of all nations the house of prayer? but ye have made it a den of thieves" (Mark 11:17). Perhaps these Greeks heard that word and were encouraged by it.

One of John's major themes is that Jesus is the Savior of the world, not simply the Redeemer of Israel. He is the Lamb of God who takes away the sin of the world (John 1:29). "For God so loved the world" (John 3:16). The Samaritans rightly identified Him as "the Savior of the world" (John 4:42). He gave His life *for* the world, and He gives life *to* the world (John 6:33). He is the Light of the World (John 8:12). The universal emphasis of John's gospel is too obvious to miss. Jesus will bring the "other sheep" who are outside the Jewish fold (John 10:16; and see 11:51–52).

The original text indicates that these Greeks "were accustomed to come and worship at the feast." They were not curious visitors or onetime investigators. No doubt they were "God-fearers," Gentiles who attended the Jewish synagogue and sought the truth, but who had not yet become proselytes. Gentiles came to see Jesus when He was a young child (Matt. 2), and now Gentiles came to see Him just before His death.

These men "kept asking" Philip for the privilege of an interview with Jesus. Philip finally told Andrew (who was often bringing people to Jesus), and Andrew gave the request to the Lord. No doubt there were many people who wanted private interviews with the Lord, but they were afraid of the Pharisees (John 9:22). Being from out of the country, the Gentile visitors either did not know about the danger or did not fear the consequences.

We can commend these Greeks for wanting to see Jesus. The Jews would say, "We would see a sign!" (Matt. 12:38; 1 Cor. 1:22), but these men said, "We would see [have an interview with] Jesus." There is no record that Jesus did talk with these men, but the message that He gave in response contains truths that all of us need.

The central theme of this message is the glory of God (John 12:23, 28). We would have expected Jesus to say, "The hour is come, that the Son of man should be crucified." But Jesus saw beyond the cross to the glory that would follow (see Luke 24:26; Heb. 12:2). In fact, the glory of God is an important theme in the remaining chapters of John's gospel (see John 13:31–32; 14:13; 17:1, 4–5, 22, 24).

Jesus used the image of a seed to illustrate the great spiritual truth that there can be no glory without suffering, no fruitful life without death, no victory without surrender. Of itself, a seed is weak and useless; but when it is planted, it "dies" and becomes fruitful. There is both beauty and bounty when a seed "dies" and fulfills its purpose. If a seed could talk, it would no doubt complain about being put into the cold, dark earth. But the only way it can achieve its goal is by being planted.

God's children are like seeds. They are small and insignificant, but they have life in them, God's life. However, that life can never be fulfilled unless we yield ourselves to God and permit Him to "plant us." We must die to self so that we may live unto God (Rom. 6; Gal. 2:20). The only way to have a fruitful life is to follow Jesus Christ in death, burial, and resurrection.

In these words, Jesus challenges us today to surrender our lives to Him. Note the contrasts: loneliness or fruitfulness; losing your life or keeping your life; serving self or serving Christ; pleasing self or receiving God's honor.

I read about some Christians who visited a remote mission station to see how the ministry was going. As they watched the dedicated missionary team at work, they were impressed with their ministry, but admitted that they missed "civilization."

"You certainly have buried yourself out here!" one of the visitors exclaimed.

"We haven't buried ourselves," the missionary replied. "We were planted!"

Our Lord knew that He was facing suffering and death, and His humanity responded to this ordeal. His soul was troubled, not because He was questioning the Father's will, but because He was fully conscious of all that the cross involved. Note that Jesus did not say, "What shall I do?" because He knew what He was ordained to do. He said, "What shall I say?" In the hour of suffering and surrender, there are only two prayers we can pray: either "Father, save me!" or "Father, glorify thy name!"

In one of my radio messages, I made the statement, "God does not expect us to be comfortable, but He does expect us to be conformable." No sooner had the program ended than my office phone rang and an anonymous listener wanted to argue with me about that statement.

"Conformable to what?" the voice thundered. "Haven't you read Romans 12:2—'Be not conformed to this world'?"

"Sure I've read Romans 12:2," I replied. "Have you read Romans 8:29? God has predestined us 'to be conformed to the image of his Son.'"

After a long pause (I was glad he was paying the phone bill), he grunted and said, "Okay."

Comfortable or *conformable*—that is the question. If we are looking for comfortable lives, then we will protect our plans and desires, save our lives, and never be planted. But if we yield our lives and let God plant us, we will never be alone but will have the joy of being fruitful to the glory of God. "If any man [Jew or Greek] serve me, let him follow me." This is the equivalent of Matthew 10:39 and Mark 8:36.

The prayer, "Father, glorify thy name!" received a reply from heaven! God the Father spoke to His Son and gave Him a double assurance: The Son's past life and ministry had glorified the Father, and the Son's future suffering and death would glorify the Father. It is significant that the Father spoke to the Son at the beginning of the Son's ministry (Matt. 3:17), as the Son began His journey to Jerusalem (Matt. 17:5), and now as the Son entered the last days before the cross. God always gives that word of assurance to those who willingly suffer for His sake.

The people heard a sound but did not know the message that had been conveyed. Yet if the voice was for their sakes and they could not understand it, what good was it? In that the voice assured Jesus, who was to die for their sakes, the voice was for their good. They heard Him pray, and they heard a sound from heaven in response to that prayer. That should have convinced them that Jesus was in touch with the Father. We might translate John 12:30, "That voice came more for your sake than for Mine."

Jesus then openly spoke about the cross. It was an hour of judgment for the world and for Satan, the prince of the world. The death of Jesus Christ would seem like a victory for the wicked world, but it would really be a judgment of the world. On the cross, Jesus would defeat Satan and his world system (Gal. 6:14). Even though he is permitted to go to and fro on the earth, Satan is a defeated enemy. As we serve the Lord, we overcome the Wicked One (Luke 10:17–19). One day Satan shall be cast out of heaven (Rev. 12:10), and eventually he will be judged and imprisoned forever (Rev. 20:10).

We have met the phrase "lifted up" before (John 3:14; 8:28). Its basic meaning is *crucifixion* (note John 12:33), but it also carries the idea of *glorification.* "Behold, My servant will prosper, He will be high and lifted up and greatly exalted" (Isa. 52:13 NASB). The Son of Man was *glorified* by being *crucified!*

The phrase "all men" does not suggest universal salvation. It means "all people without distinction," that is, Jews and Gentiles. He does not force them; He draws them (see John 6:44–45). He was "lifted up" that people might find the way (John 12:32), know the truth (John 8:28), and receive the life (John 3:14). The cross reminds us that God loves the whole world and that the task of the church is to take the gospel to the whole world.

The people did not understand what He was teaching. They knew that "Son of man" was a title for Messiah, but they could not understand why the Messiah would be crucified! Did not the Old Testament teach that the Messiah would live forever? (See Ps. 72:17; 89:36; 110:4; Isa. 9:7.)

But that was no time to be discussing the finer points of theology! It was an hour of crisis (see John 12:31, where the Greek word *krisis* means judgment) and an hour of opportunity. The light was shining, and they had better take advantage of their opportunity to be saved! We have met this image of light and darkness before (John 1:4–9; 3:17–20; 8:12; 9:39–41). By a simple step of faith, these people could have passed out of spiritual darkness and into the light of salvation.

This marked the end of our Lord's public ministry as far as John's record is concerned. Jesus departed and hid Himself. It was judgment on the nation that saw His miracles, heard His messages, and scrutinized His ministry and yet refused to believe in Him.

4. JESUS AND UNBELIEVING JEWS (12:37–49)

The key word in this section is *believe;* it is used eight times. First, John explained the unbelief of the people. They *would not* believe (John 12:37–38, with a quotation from Isa. 53:1); they *could not* believe (John 12:39); and they *should not* believe (John 12:40–41, with a quotation from Isa. 6:9–10).

In spite of all the clear evidence that was presented to them, the Jews would not believe. The "arm of the Lord" had been revealed to them in great power, yet they closed their eyes to the truth. They had heard the message ("report") and seen the miracles and yet would not believe.

When a person starts to resist the light, something begins to change within him, and he comes to the place where he cannot believe. There is "judicial blindness" that God permits to come over the eyes of people who do not take the truth seriously. (The quotation of Isa. 6:9–10 is found in a number of places in the New Testament. See Matt. 13:14–15; Mark 4:12; Luke 8:10; Acts 28:25–27; Rom. 11:8.) It is a serious thing to treat God's truth lightly, for a person could well miss his opportunity to be saved. "Seek ye the LORD while he may be found, call ye upon him while he is near" (Isa. 55:6).

There were those who would not believe, and there were those who would not openly confess Christ even though they had believed (John 12:42–43). Nicodemus and Joseph of Arimathea belonged to this group initially but eventually came out openly in their confession of Christ (John 19:38ff.). In the early church, there were numbers of Pharisees (Acts 15:5) and even priests (Acts 6:7). It was the old struggle between the glory of God and the praise of people (John 12:25–26). It was a costly thing to be excommunicated (John 9:22), and these "secret believers" wanted the best of both worlds. Note John 5:44 in this regard.

In John 12:44–50 we have our Lord's last message before He "hid himself" from the people. Again, the emphasis was on faith. A number of the basic themes in John's gospel run through this message: God sent the Son; to see the Son means to see the Father; Jesus is the Light of the World; His words are the very words of God; faith in Him brings salvation;

to reject Him is to face eternal judgment. In fact, the very Word that He spoke will judge those who have rejected it and Him!

It is an awesome thought that the unbeliever will face at the judgment every bit of Scripture he has ever read or heard. The very Word that he rejects becomes his judge! Why? Because the written Word points to the Living Word, Jesus Christ (John 1:14).

Many people reject the truth simply because of the fear of people (John 12:42–43). Among those who will be in hell are "the fearful" (Rev. 21:8). Better to fear God and go to heaven than to fear people and go to hell!

The word *judge* is repeated four times in the closing words of this message, and a solemn word it is. Jesus did not come to judge; He came to save (John 3:18; 8:15). But if the sinner will not trust the Savior, the Savior must become the Judge. The sinner is actually passing judgment on himself or herself, not on the Lord!

As you have studied these twelve chapters of the gospel of John, you have seen Jesus Christ in His life, His ministry, His miracles, His message, and His desire to save lost sinners.

You have considered the evidence. Have you come to the conviction that Jesus Christ is indeed the Son of God, the Savior of the world?

Have *you* trusted Him and received everlasting life?

"While you have the light, believe in the light, that you may become sons of light" (John 12:36 NKJV).

QUESTIONS FOR PERSONAL REFLECTION
OR GROUP DISCUSSION

1. When has God seemed to act out of character or done something you weren't expecting Him to do? How did you feel?

2. Read verses 1–11. If you had been at this dinner, would you have been more likely to be Martha (the worker), Mary (the extravagant worshipper), Lazarus (the living evidence of Jesus' power), or Judas (the traitor). Explain.

3. Why do you think Mary anointed Jesus' feet with her perfume?

4. Do you think Mary knew that Jesus' burial was going to be soon (v. 7)? Why or why not?

5. How do you think Mary's gift made Jesus feel?

6. Does verse 8 mean that money should be spent on worship rather than on the poor? Explain how you understand this verse.

7. Read verses 12–19. What was the crowd expecting Jesus to do when He rode into Jerusalem?

8. Read verses 20–36. What did Jesus mean by what He said in verses 24–25?

9. In what ways did Jesus not do what was expected of Him?

10. Read verses 37–50. What did Jesus teach about faith in this last speech before hiding Himself from the people?

11. How can you respond when God acts in ways contrary to what you would choose or expect?

The "BE" series . . .

For years pastors and lay leaders have embraced Warren W. Wiersbe's very accessible commentary of the Bible through the individual "BE" series. Through the work of David C. Cook Global Mission, the "BE" series is part of a library of books made available to indigenous Christian workers. These are men and women who are called by God to grow the kingdom through their work with the local church worldwide. Here are a few of their remarks as to how Dr. Wiersbe's writings have benefited their ministry.

"Most Christian books I see are priced too high for me . . .
I received a collection that included 12 Wiersbe
commentaries a few months ago and I have
read every one of them.
I use them for my personal devotions every day and they
are incredibly helpful for preparing sermons.
The contribution David C. Cook is making to the
church in India is amazing."
—Pastor E. M. Abraham, Hyderabad, India

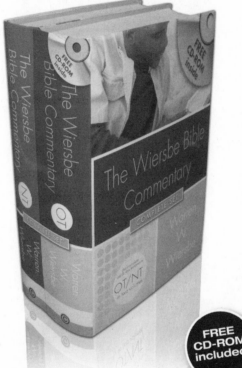

TOURNAMENT
TROUBLE

SYLV CHIANG

Art by CONNIE CHOI

Designed by Kong Njo

Annick Press Ltd.

We acknowledge the support of the Canada Council for the Arts and the Ontario Arts Council, and the participation of the Government of Canada/ la participation du gouvernement du Canada for our publishing activities.

ONTARIO ARTS COUNCIL
CONSEIL DES ARTS DE L'ONTARIO
an Ontario government agency
un organisme du gouvernement de l'Ontario

Cataloging in Publication

Chiang, Sylv, author
    Tournament trouble / Sylv Chiang ; art by Connie Choi.

(Cross ups ; 1)
Issued in print and electronic formats.
ISBN 978-1-77321-009-4 (hardcover).–ISBN 978-1-77321-008-7 (softcover).–
ISBN 978-1-77321-011-7 (PDF).–ISBN 978-1-77321-010-0 (EPUB)

    I. Choi, Connie, illustrator II. Title.

. PS8605.H522T68 2018   jC813'.6   C2017-905512-7
                                                       C2017-905513-5

Published in the U.S.A. by Annick Press (U.S.) Ltd.
Distributed in Canada by University of Toronto Press.
Distributed in the U.S.A. by Publishers Group West.

Printed in Canada

annickpress.com
connie-choi.com
Follow Sylv Chiang on Twitter @SylvChiang

Also available as an e-book. Please visit www.annickpress.com/ebooks.html for more details.